Yana
252-9763

SO THE KIDS ARE REVOLTING . . . ?

SO THE KIDS ARE REVOLTING . . . ?

A Game Plan for Jewish
(and All Other) Parents

ALBERT VORSPAN

1970
DOUBLEDAY & COMPANY, INC., GARDEN CITY, NEW YORK

Library of Congress Catalog Card Number 70–116907
Copyright © 1970 by Albert Vorspan
All Rights Reserved
Printed in the United States of America
First Edition

CONTENTS

"The parents have eaten sour grapes and the children's teeth are on edge."

(Jeremiah 31:29)

PREFACE

I got into a bit of trouble with some of my coreligionists with my last book, *My Rabbi Doesn't Make House Calls*, especially when one reviewer inadvertently titled the book, *My Rabbi Doesn't Make Housewives!*

So I considered using a pen name for this book. The name I thought of was Philip Roth. That way I would have gotten off the hook and had a best seller in one fell swoop. My publisher nixed the idea, so here I am once again with my own name, my own book and the product of a sharp pencil, a big mouth and beaucoup *chutzpah*.

This book is dedicated to my wife, Shirley, and our four children—Chuck, Robby, Kenny and Debby—whose loving support and frank criticism were invaluable and a royal pain in the neck. I welcomed their generous suggestions and, as you see, decided to go ahead with this book anyway.

I also wish to thank Rabbi Alexander Schindler, who makes house calls, for his generous advice and counsel; Ruth Harrison and Vivian Mendeles for their patience in putting my hieroglyphics into typescript; and Doubleday for their insouciance. These are tense times—laughter and joy do not come easily. But humor is a necessary safety valve, preserving our sanity in a mad world.

Albert Vorspan
Hewlett, Long Island, New York
January 1, 1970

SO THE KIDS ARE REVOLTING . . . ?

CHAPTER ONE

HOW TO ENJOY WORRYING

Jews are the world's greatest worriers. Thanks to the tender, loving care of Christians throughout twenty millennia, we have had a great deal to worry about. But worrying for two thousand years finally becomes a habit, an ingredient of personality, and it persists even in rare moments when—or perhaps especially when—there is not much to worry about. Why are things so good? Why is everything so quiet? What's wrong? If things are too good, it's no doubt bad for the Jews, but don't worry sometimes—God will provide.

Today Jewish worries are blooming again. And there is plenty to worry about—Israel, Russian Jewry, anti-Semitism in many places, including the United States. So what are Jews worrying about? Their children, that's what. Jewish children in America are not starving, or selling apples or digging in mines far away from the sun. No, they are healthy, sun-tanned, live in nice homes in fine neighborhoods and they go to the best colleges in the country. Ah, but that's the rub. College, as one worried Jewish pundit has proclaimed, is a "disaster area" for Jewish life and Jewish values. And since 85 per cent of Jewish college-age youngsters are indeed on the college campus (compared with 20 per cent for Catholics and 35 per cent for Protestants), and one wag defines a Jewish drop-out as a lad with a terminal Master's Degree, we have a soul-sized worry. And we don't throw away such a worry.

In one sense, Jewish worrying about youth shares in the general American worrying about youth. We must all be reminded that youth today do what youth have *always* done—grow up, fall in love, get married, live together and have children. It's just the ORDER that's different today. And Jewish parents share with all others an anxiety about crazy styles of hair, clothes, bathing habits, drugs, college violence and far-out life-styles. Today the colleges serve in *loco parentis* (which is Latin for "let them drive the professors crazy like they did their parents").

But for Jews there is a special hang-up: Will we "lose" our youth to Judaism? Will our sons and daughters become so pre-occupied with the occupation of buildings that they will forget about their Jewish identity? Will they be so stoned that they will abandon the rock of their faith? Will they be so charged up about black studies and black identity that they will neglect their JEWISH identity? While the Hadassah women are inside the temple buying Israel Bonds, will their kids be outside selling Al Fatah stamps? Will they campaign for pot in every chicken? When the boys are bearded, barefoot and sad-eyed, won't they look just like Jesus? Will they be so involved in fighting the Establishment that they will spit in the face of the Jewish Establishment, too? To all these questions, the answer is: Probably! So worry.

For example, you can get plenty of mileage worrying about your son's first year at college. After all, away from home for the first time, rooming in a cubicle with a Druid ("but you don't look Druish") farmer who gets up at three o'clock each morning to jog to the bathroom, and with all the problems of adjustment to a new and strange way of life, it is not surprising that your boy experiences the freshman blues, followed in rapid order by the sophomore slump, the junior slump and the senior slump, at each stage of which he transfers, of course, to another college. Without funky parents like you worrying to death about him, he would get along equally poorly. But *you* would be miserable!

Jewish worries about our college students did not begin with this generation or even this country. Jews cannot make it without the university—for us it is the gateway to success. Sholom Aleichem's poignant story, "The Gymnasium," while set in Czarist Russia, is hauntingly contemporary. After years of heartbreaking struggle to get his son into a university in the face of anti-Jewish quotas and bitter daily indignities, Aaron Katz finds that his son isn't going to school any more; the students are on strike! Proudly the boy tells his father how he and his Gentile classmates are fighting against injustice. Aaron weeps: "It was for this I sacrificed myself? So that you could go out on strike? May God protect us. Who will suffer for it? We Jews!"

You can also worry sometimes whether you were born into the right century. What's with this twentieth century anyway? You call this a century when about the only good thing that happened was the birth of Israel, the death of Hitler and the Miracle of the Mets? You call this a century when you ask your son what he is taking at college and he replies the Administration Building and the Chem Lab, and you are AFRAID to ask your daughter what SHE is taking? This is by you YOUR century?

Personally, I think we would have been better off if we had been incarnated in an earlier, more placid century—an easier time in which to raise one's children. Say, for example, thirteenth-century Europe. What could be bad—chivalry, Magna Carta, round tables and good knights, peasants under glass, riding to hunt, royalty, the whole shmeer? And yet—mark this well—in that very century, students seized control of the University of Bologna and the University of Paris, put all professors on short leashes and under the absolute control of a smart-alecky student rector—a kind of juvenile Mayor Daley. No professor could even go to King John without permission, and all decisions on curriculum were made by the students, all power to the people. What happened? Student power was a shambles, realizing which, the students restored irrelevant classes and unresponsive adult administration and lived happily ever after in the pre-Columbian age. So much for the thirteenth! Anybody for the fifteenth?

Some of our contemporary young mystics really *believe* in reincarnation and walk the streets making eye-contact with cats they are sure they knew in previous incarnations. ("I can't place your face, but I definitely remember the century.")

We have, obviously, a great deal to worry about. But, in typical Jewish fashion, we should try to isolate our worries, break them down and examine them rationally—one by one.

Are we worried that our young ones will abandon the faith of
their fathers? *Nu*, so what else is new? Didn't our generation
do that, too? Maybe every generation has done it—even Moses'
followers kept ducking out of the line of march to try to sneak
back to Egypt. But Judaism is still around—seen any Philistines
lately? If they are anything like we were, they will abandon,
they will run, they will doubt and they will repudiate—until
they marry and the children come and the question is: Where
do we send the kids to get a Jewish education, they should
know they are Jewish!

But, on the other hand, we can also worry about this: In
their condemnation of our ways, what if they are right? What
if they are right that our generation of Americans has helped
to mess up America and the world, that making a living is not
the same as making a life, that religion has become a mere
ornament of the status quo, and that we adults have lost sight
of purpose and meaning and human community, and that most
of us lead driven but empty lives? What if they are right
about *that*? Then the least they can do is keep their big mouths
shut. After all, it is *we*—and not *they*—who have scrimped and
saved, so it is we—and not they—who are the *saving remnant*.

One thing is certain. We will never be satisfied with him
(or her), so we will always have plenty to worry about. We will
not be satisfied if he lets his hair grow to the floor, but also
not if he is the only crew-cut jock in the university. Not if he
is one of those eager-beaver bookworms, but also not if he care-
lessly glides through school on the skin of his teeth, uncon-
taminated by any book whatsoever. Not if he quickly gets
deeply involved with just one girl ("I mean, how can you
develop a standard unless you meet lots of girls?"), but also
not if he flits from chick to chick like an adolescent chicken-
flicker with acne. Not if he is thin, but also not if he is fat.
Not if he makes up his mind too quickly about his future
career, and also not if he doesn't have the foggiest where he is
going in life.

Not if he is "too Jewish" (refusing to eat Chinese food is
"too Jewish"), but also not if he is "anti-Jewish" (criticizing
Israel is "anti-Jewish"). Not if he wants to go to college a
thousand miles away in Yennavelt, Missouri, but also not if
he wants to stay home and commute. Not if he is alienated,

but also not if he is conformist. Not if he is stoned, but also not if he is a bluenosed vitamin.

But, you may say, these are the extremes! What about the happy medium, the good old in-between, a leetle moderation? Forget it, dear reader, the middle way is fast disappearing. In a time of polarization, you cannot dance at two weddings at the same time.

So there is much to worry about. The question is not what to worry about. The harder question is: How? How worry? There are many ways to worry, but they are not equally effective or contemporary.

1 INTERNAL

One way is to internalize all your anxiety. Bottle the tension inside of you like seltzer water. Be cheerful on the outside and tearful (and carbonated) on the inside. If somebody asks if anything is wrong, look at your shoes and say solemnly: "Don't ask!" This method of worrying is brave and selfless, keeps you from inflicting your *tsores* on everyone else, gives you a nice feeling of martyred rectitude and keeps your weight down because you are an injustice collector and eat very little besides your heart out. Which, for many internalized worriers, keeps them happy indeed.

2 EXTERNAL

The externalized worrier shares his worries with everyone, regardless of race, color or creed. This way, unlike the internal, you will not get ulcers; you will *give* them. Why should you have to shoulder a bag of worries all by yourself? Share the miseries. Stop strangers on the street. Seize each one by the elbow and open the conversation with: "Listen, you think *you've* got troubles?" which is a pretty good attention-grabbing opener. Then, before he can flee, bang his ear about your children, the state of the world or the price of watercress—whichever is bugging you at the moment. Just as human wealth is badly maldistributed, so is what to worry. Some poor deprived souls have nothing. You have a surplus. So you, single-handedly, will redress the balance, afflict the comfortable and spread tsores around with the abandon of the old Rockefeller passing out shiny dimes like the weird WASP he was.

3   THE MIDDLE WAY

The middle way, fast disappearing, is neither to internalize or externalize. It is to *kvetch* a little and sigh a lot. The Gentile sigh is pronounced "oh"; the Jewish sigh is pronounced "oy." In the penultimate worry, it comes out "oy, gvalt!" Which is an untranslatable summary of three thousand years of worry.

Does it do any good to worry about our young people? It does little, if any, good for the young people, but it might give *us* a *raison d'être*, a *modus vivendi* and a full way of life. Not to mention, of course, this timely book which is frankly only for those who have children, plan to have children, or *were* children.

This book is designed to help you cope with your young person from the cradle to the campus. You'll need patience, *mazel* (luck), a Yiddishe *kop* and a sense of humor (humor is the Jewish way to discharge anxiety: we laugh in order not to cry) regardless of your race, religion, creed or national origin.

Remember, youth must be served—maybe with apples in their mouths? It's just a stage. So, don't worry sometimes.

CHAPTER TWO

HOW TO EXPLAIN TO HIM—WHY BE JEWISH?

*If it's good enough for God, it's good enough for
him (with a small "h").*

Keeping Harold Jewish from the cradle to the campus (and
beyond if possible) is a constant challenge. Throughout his
youth, Harold will bug you with the question: Why be Jewish?
Don't duck the question. You want him to learn about it in
the streets? Face it squarely. Explain things to him. He should
know that being Jewish is the process of spending one's life
asking: what does it mean to be Jewish?

Begin by telling him how much Jews have suffered. Tell him
how Jews have been persecuted for thousands of years. With
deep pathos, recite the countless ways that Jews have been
tormented and destroyed at the hands of the anti-Semites
through all the dread centuries. When this does not seem to get
a rise out of him, recall the experiences of your own childhood,
the beatings and daily harassments you suffered at the hands
of Jew-baiting hoodlums. When the desired response is still not
forthcoming (the desired response, by the way, is: "*Hineni*
[Here am I], send me," but your Harold can't even speak
Hebrew and wouldn't volunteer to walk one block to the Dairy
Barn), you will add: "Not only *that*. Did you ever hear of the
Depression? Did you know that my very family was on *relief*
—what you call *welfare*? Did you know *that*, dammit; you think
it was a lot of laughs growing up Jewish?" By now, your tone
is quite bellicose, and Harold is beginning to feel vaguely responsible for your suffering. His eyes are getting glassy and he

is thinking to himself: *This* is why I should be Jewish, but what if I don't *like* to suffer? And Harold is obviously planning the quickest possible exit from this rap.

"Listen, Harold," you blurt out, "you're so damn smart. Let me tell you there is plenty of anti-Semitism today, too—in Russia, in Poland, in South America, and don't think it can't happen *here* either. I say, scratch a Gentile and you'll find an anti-Semite!"

"Aw, come off it, Dad," Harold says. "You don't really believe that! I'm fifteen years old—and I've never experienced anti-Semitism yet. How can you put everybody into bags—them and us, Jews and anti-Semites? How can you generalize like that? You know what you are, Dad? You're a *bigot*, for Christ sake, and YOU THINK THIS IS WHY I SHOULD BE JEWISH?"

So, there you have it, man. The suffering approach got you nowhere, except a little more suffering on your part. Not only did you strike out, in the end, as is the game plan of the young; he succeeded in putting you down, making YOU the villain of the piece. You thought you could use the heavy weapon of anti-Semitism to beat some Jewish loyalty into him, but what happened? He turns you, the eternal victim, into a bigot, of all things, and by now you are beginning to realize that the negative approach ("because our forefathers died, that's why") is not an effective answer to why be Jewish. So shift gears. Think positively.

Explain to him that the Old Testament provided the cement of Western civilization and that most radical thinkers in human history—Freud, Marx and Einstein—were Jewish. You can tell him that Jews make a significant contribution to the cultural *élan* and the social conscience of American life. You can tell him about the disproportionate number of Jewish Nobel prize winners, letting drop how C. P. Snow, who isn't even Jewish, thinks Jews have "superior genes." Put this down as a "Snow job" because your son will reject, as he should, all talk of racial superiority, even Jewish, and will laugh at the picture of Jews swimming around in an exclusive gene pool in Atlantic City. But why were so many of the kids who went to Mississippi to fight racial segregation Jews? Why do Jews vote liberal? Why are so many Jewish young people involved in campus causes and the social ferment? The answer: because they are shaped by a Jewish value system which comes from our history and our religious faith, because only one with a broken heart can be a whole man and the Jewish heart was broken so Jews could be a blessing unto all mankind. Explain it to him.

If that doesn't grab him, explain that the Old Testament —that's the Jewish Bible, baby—is a yeasty record of protest and rebellion. Recent archaeological discoveries in the Middle East demonstrate, strikingly, unparalleled parallels. Abraham broke his father's idols; Samson grew his hair like a muscle-bound hippie and Delilah cut it off in the middle of the night like an uptight Jewish mother; Joshua demonstrated at Jericho; the Maccabees were guerrilla fighters; and David knocked off both Goliath (who was stoned) and Bathsheba (who was built); the prophets ran around with hair down to their *pupiks* and wearing Pillsbury flour sacks; the Israelites ate soul food in the desert; and Adam told Eve, "Look, honey, we're living at a time of transition and we gotta do our own thing." The Talmud says: "Who can protest and does not is an accomplice." Old Moses was the model of an angry Jewish youth, even though he was on the dark side of middle age before he got cracking and had to put down the young rebel, Korah, in the process. . . .

This Hebrew cat, Moses, started in adversity. As a baby, he was up the creek without a paddle. Drawn by some Egyptian chicks out of the floating wicker bag, Moses' first words were, allegedly: "That's not *my* bag." He was raised in the suburban palace of the Pharaoh, eating curds and whey and denouncing white racism. He was an advocate of non-violence until the day he saw a soul brother being manhandled by an Egyptian cop. Moses blew his cool, shouted something about Jewish Power and slew the Egyptian on the spot. After that, non-violence was no longer his thing. Freedom was. Freedom Now. Not with all deliberate speed. But NOW. Moses became a leader despite the murmuring of his followers: "By what authority? Who died and left him boss? Who is this Moses cat? What kind of a name is *that* for a Jewish boy, anyway? I wouldn't follow HIM anywhere! I'd rather be a slave in Egypt than to have to listen to another one of his stammering speeches. Wow, man, he talks like he's got a mouthful of knishes!"

So this cat, Moses, drawing his strength from the people, appointed a committee (himself and his brother Aaron) and decided to confront the Pharaoh Establishment. Bursting into the palace while the Pharaoh was signing a contract to sell more bricks, hewn by Hebrew slaves, to the Egyptian military-industrial combine, Moses occupied the Sphinx Room of the palace and proclaimed the following non-negotiable demand: "Let my people go . . . or up against the wall, Pharaoh!"

Pharaoh, over thirty-five years old and stubborn like all establishments, rejected Moses' demand out of hand. "Who are you to come in here and present non-negotiable demands? Who gave you the right to speak for the Hebrew slaves anyway? Did you ever have to meet a payroll? I have a letter from the Uncle Tom Committee of Hebrew Slaves in Support of the Pharaoh and of Hebrew Slavery! They say you do not speak for them. Such chutzpah you have! I am responsible to my Board of Trustees, one of the most responsible bodies in all of Egypt, not to long-haired Hebrew rebels storming in here without an appointment and uttering threats against me and my nation . . . anyway, what do you mean 'or else'? Huh?"

Pharaoh found out what Moses meant. The plagues socked it to him. Boils, frogs, pot, beads, sickness, meetings, beards and dirty feet, bad commercials, bad vibrations. Pharaoh went on national television, denouncing Moses as an "effete snob" and demanding that he be investigated by the un-Egyptian Affairs Committee.

Moses, rebellious and full of pith and vinegar, spoke pithily to Pharaoh through a bullhorn: "We leave at dawn, whether you agree or not! We are armed with the might of God and we will not hesitate to use all our weapons. So, you're up against the wall, baby!"

Don't tell Harold the rest of the story because it is out of sight and he will never believe it anyway, especially about the Red Sea and later, at Sinai, where Moses says: "God, don't dictate so fast." Enough is enough.

If that doesn't impress him, try another tack. Take a deep breath and explain to him that God is also Jewish, so why shouldn't Harold relax and enjoy it?

One shrewd way to prove to him that God is Jewish is to begin with the basic premise of Christian theology. If Jesus, whose Jewishness is universally acknowledged, was the son of God, then wasn't God Jewish? Not necessarily. In Jewish law the child is the religion of the mother. Mary must have been Jewish because she insisted on her son's circumcision, and the American Jewish Yearbook of the pre-Christian era says nothing about God being married to a *shiksa*.

But must Jews accept Christian theology in order to prove that God is Jewish? No. While it is true that God does not look Jewish, there is much internal evidence to show that He was and is. In the first place, He gave the law to Moses in the mountains. Why the mountains? Why not at the Temple in Jerusalem? Why not at the Dan Carmel in Haifa? Why not at the Pierre? Because only a Jewish God would know that in the heat of the summer His people would not be in the temple, but would hie themselves to the mountains. Secondly, God offered the Jews a land of milk and honey, not a land of beer and pretzels, wine and cheese, fish and chips or pizza and beer. Thirdly, He revealed himself through a holy book, not through a TV program, a sonata or a coliseum circus or work of art. Fourthly, He was always sending his loved ones on errands (Jonah to Nineveh; Abraham to Canaan; Moses to the Promised Land, etc.), all the while rebuking them for being ungrateful pups who never appreciated all that was done for them. Fifthly, He was always comparing them to their neighbors. ("Are ye not like the Ethiopians unto Me?") And, also, He was forever hocking His people about what He did for them in the olden days about which they couldn't care less. ("Where were thou when I laid the foundations of the world? . . .") And who but a Jewish father would permit so much back talk and fresh lip from his sons and, though always threatening to zap them, loved them nonetheless and rarely lifted a hand to belt even the most insolent? Thus it is clear God was—and is—Jewish. So what? That is a good question.

Is it possible that the hard knocks Jews have endured throughout their history stem precisely from the Jewishness of God? After all, a Jewish God, who is of course at the same time a God of all mankind, would bend over backward to avoid showing favoritism to his fellow Jews? Didn't Ambassador Goldberg cry less about Israel than Hubert Humphrey did? When you take the neighborhood kids to the beach, aren't you more severe with your own? Would the Gentiles respect a God who was always pulling Jewish chestnuts out of the fire? Wouldn't that be cosmic nepotism? It isn't that God has forgotten His Jewish children; it may be that He just got worn down by all those committee meetings. Deep theological questions, indeed, but there are still more profound issues at stake.

If God is Jewish, where does that leave Christians and other believers? They could, of course, worship a Jewish God, but their ambivalence toward Jews would constantly distort their faith. After all, what would a Jewish God think of the goings on in Rome about deicide, the tsimmes about birth control, marrying priests, Protestant churches drowned in leaking guilt? Christianity might well argue that the Father was Jewish, but was so angered by the mean way Jews treated His son that He converted to Christianity. But that wouldn't help too much since Christians' ambivalence is so deep that, even after a thousand generations they would still refer to a convert, even God, as "our Jewish friend." And even if God did convert to Christianity, if He died, Jews would sit *shiva* and rend their sackcloths.

What if God is Jewish? What difference does it make? It may help to explain why Jews tend to be so secular and irreligious. If God was definitely a Christian, Jews would be more impressed. They would try to keep up with the Joneses and the McCarthys. But with a Jewish God, Jews will always find fault: "He never talks to us any more. He doesn't talk our language. He doesn't understand modern ways. He lives in the past. He expects too much of us. He is just too square. He has His life and we have ours. He's become very Establishment. He's never satisfied. We still love Him, but you know He's too old to live with us any more. He's better off by Himself."

There is another implication. If God is Jewish, that is another burden He must carry. It is enough tsores to be God without being Jewish as well—and vice versa. Today it is "in" to be Jewish (perhaps for only a brief moment—Chinese, Mexicans, homosexuals and Indians are crowding in and will soon eclipse us). But God should not be a fashionable God, an ornament of the latest fad. God should be a Great Demand, inherently alienated from every culture. But when everything and everybody becomes Jewish by osmosis, what is so unique about a Jewish God? God should be a non-conformist, and He might do better as a Jehovah's Witness, a southern Baptist, a High Episcopalian female Negro or a student radical. Jews are *in* and God must be *out!* If God becomes a culture hero, as Jews have done, He will be as dead as the Protestant obituaries have tried to make Him.

So what is to be done? We must ask the National Conference of Christians and Jews to make God non-sectarian. This would be the ultimate denouement of the thrust toward ecumania. The Vatican Council could have another big meeting and solemnly declare that the Father is non-sectarian. This would cause a religious revival among Jews and all other ecumaniacs. God, of course, might get so fed up with the prospect of another millennium of Brotherhood dinners and dialogues that He might well unleash the escatalogical fire this time, but if it is a non-sectarian God who is at fault, at least it won't provoke the anti-Semites.

Of course, if Harold doesn't believe in God either, this exegesis will not do you, God or Harold much good. In that case, the best answer to why be Jewish is the Israeli answer: *"Ein b'rerah,"* which means roughly: "You have a choice?"

CHAPTER THREE

HOW TO NAME THE CHILD—
THE NAME OF THE GAME

Now that you have had a mere glimpse (believe me) of the problems, you will realize that it is never too early to worry about your child. Keeping your child Jewish must start at birth, if not before. (If he gets alienated in infancy, he will have nothing to look forward to.) The baby is probably stuck with your last—or family—name, whatever it is, but—now that you have sent away for the college catalogues, belatedly nailed a *mezuzah* on the doorpost, and hired a sure-fingered *mohel* for the *bris* (circumcision) eight days hence (brit control) —you'd better settle on a good Jewish first name for the boy (I mean, it *is* a boy, isn't it?).

A generation ago many Jews, experiencing anti-Semitism, changed their noses and their family names to try to "pass as *goyim*." (*Then* we said: "Why can't *we* be like *them?*" Today we say: "Why can't *they* be like *us?*") Jews are now sufficiently secure in their Jewishness and in American pluralism to regard changing the family name as an unworthy self-denial, a kind of assimilation on the cheap. "If I am not for myself, who will be for me?" our sages asked. Maybe the family does not have a coat of arms, a family seal or a clearly defined family tree to climb around on (the Rothchilds used to have a red shield on their home and the Adlers an eagle), but how many families can trace their lineage to Abraham, Moses, David and Jeremiah?

In Biblical times, names conveyed certain characteristics or experiences. The name "Isaac" flows from the Hebrew word for laughter because Sarah, wife of Abraham, burst into laughter when she learned she would bear a son at the unlikely age of ninety. The variety of names is evident in the fact that one finds very few repeats in the long list of "begats" in the Bible —our forefathers looked upon each child as unique. During most of Jewish history, Jews did not have surnames. Surnames in addition to given names appeared among Sephardic Jews in the Middle Ages. Among Ashkenazic Jews, surnames appear to have become common in the eighteenth century. The Austrian Government issued a decree in 1787, requiring Jews to adopt surnames.

And when, not so many generations ago, we acquired family names, usually there was nothing Jewish about them. Mostly, they were copied from the non-Jewish surroundings in which they originated.* Our Jewish forefathers often borrowed vocational names: A shoemaker became Shuster; a printer became Drucker; a tailor, Schneider; a merchant, Kaufman; miller, Miller; gardener, Gartner; a jeweler, Goldsmith. We are not certain whether a painter became Paintner nor how Sam Schmuckler got his name (although there is a suspicion he had to bribe an official for the last three letters).

Many Jews got their names from the map. Such family names as Berlin, Warsaw, Danzig, Halpern, Posner (from the city of Posen), Brody, Horowitz, Ginsberg sprang right from the accidents of geography. In other cases, anti-Jewish officials afflicted their Jewish subjects with such names as Eselkopf (donkey's head) and Fresser (glutton). Thus, most of the names we now think of as so Jewish have non-Jewish origins. Names that end in "vich" are Russian, "sohn" is German, "ski" is Polish. So what's Jewish about Jewish family names? Cohen and Levy may be the only completely Jewish names among us.

In America, many Jewish family names were born in the minds of baffled immigration inspectors at Ellis Island, who

* Much of the factual data in this chapter is drawn from an article by Maurice Cohen, *United Synagogue Review*, Summer, 1969.

couldn't make head or tail out of the pidgin English of the frightened Jewish immigrant. The American immigration inspectors probably christened more Jews than all the missionaries in history. A classic story is of the puzzled Jewish immigrant, about to be admitted into the Golden Medinah of America, who was confronted by a harried Ellis Island inspector who demanded to know the immigrant's name. Overwhelmed and confused, the immigrant threw up his hands and cried "Shain Fargessen!" (Yiddish for "I forgot already!"). Satisfied, the inspector filled out the form and ushered newly named Shane Ferguson into his beloved America.

Against this background, one should not be too harsh on those Jewish people who decided to change their names from Rabinowitz to Raab, from Robert Zimmerman to Bob Dylan, from Liebowitz to Lee, from Kaplan to Capp, from Smolinowitz to Stone, from Bernglasser to Burn, from Kantzipper to Kant, from Pillar to Post. Basically, Goldberg and Schwartz are no more Jewish than Powell and Janesbury. So there is no disgrace in cutting one's name down to a size which can fit on a sheet of paper or trip off the tongue without breaking the teeth.

No, it is the mangling of the *first* name that must give pause. The Bible says, "Now these are the names of the sons of Israel who came into Egypt . . . Reuben, Simeon, Levi and Judah." Our sages did not deign to jazz up their names in Egypt. Reuben and Judah came on in Egypt as Reuben and Judah. No matter how uncomfortable or uncongenial the environment into which they wandered, Jews persisted in holding onto their peculiarly Jewish names. The rabbis went so far as to observe that this was one of the characteristics that earned for the Israelites salvation and redemption.

But here, in the free soil of America, we are throwing all this away. At the same time as it has now become kosher to preserve the Jewish *family* name, we Jews are now wont to saddle our children with *trefe* first names (and middle names) that have no resemblance to anything Jewish, past or present, living or dead. It is as if the Jewish home has become a fortress over which we proudly fly the Jewish flag, but inside the fortress any connection between what we call each other and our Hebrew (or Jewish) character is, largely, coincidental.

The current generation of Jewish youth is spearheaded by
the following:

Rex	Christopher	Sharon
Blake	Lori	Shad
Brad	Marci	Sherri
Chad	Margo	Tami
Cindy	Lance	Toni
Debbi	Patti	Vicki
Judi	Scott	Wayne
Kathi	Dawn	Wendi

So what's Jewish about these names? Why are we permitting
assimilation at the head while resisting it at the tail? What if
we save our Jewish soul food and lose our Jewish names?
Shakespeare may ask what's in a name, but we must respond:
Jewish survival, that's what. The time has come to put a stop
to aping the Gentiles and letting Hollywood and television soap
operas inspire the names we give our children. The time has
come to stop pretending that we are fulfilling our Jewish responsibility by giving our children auxiliary names in Hebrew
(which they do not even try to remember until *bar mitzvah*
and, later, the wedding) while sticking them with milk-and-
water, pretty-pretty, Americanized names which possess neither
character nor Jewish significance. Better for Liebowitz to become Lee but continue as Reuben than to hang onto Liebowitz and become Rex.

A Jewish flavor to a name, redolent with history and meaning,
can have a subtle, but no less real, impact upon his psyche. It
may contribute in a positive and emotional way to the Jewish
identity, which you properly want so much for him to retain.
(So why is your first name Henry instead of Hillel, or Toni instead of Tamar? If a reactionary goyish Congressman from
South Carolina can be Mendel (Rivers), you could at least
be Isaiah!) Forget the bloodless names proposed in the baby
books. Ignore the antiseptically euphonious marquee names.
Consider the following names which reflect yiddishkeit and an
aromatic Jewish blend in a world in which the bland lead the
bland. Here are some names which stir memories, both ancient

and recent, rekindling the glories of our history and, equally,
the mystery of the Hebrew present and future:

Aaron	David	Rebecca
Abraham	Gideon	Ruth
Abram	Haddassah	Seth
Adam	Hillel	Tamara
Avinoam	Isaiah	Tziporah
Aviva	Joshua	Yaacov
	Naomi	Alexander*

*(personally I don't think this name has got it, but did you know
that every male Jewish child born in Jerusalem in 332 BCE
was named "Alexander" in honor of the visit there by Alexander
the Great—and that one of my good friends from Westport is
named Alexander and begged to be listed here?)

I would also like to recommend that we restore a beautiful
ancient custom which goes back two thousand years. In those
days, a tree was planted upon the birth of a child—pine or
cypress for a girl, cedar for a boy, symbolizing the hope that
the youngster would grow like a young tree. Later, when the
child was grown and ready for marriage, the trunk of the tree
was used to build the *chupah* (marriage canopy) in accordance
with the Biblical verse, "How goodly are thy tends, O Jacob,
thy dwellings, O Israel" (Numbers 24:4).

And you went and named him Harold! Not only will he
hate it, but now you will feel guilty about it and he will
drive you up the tree with chutzpah but without the *chupah*
and it serves you right! So go ahead and mail out the birth
announcement already:

Mr. and Mrs._____
proudly inform you of the birth of
their son, Harold, the doctor. . . .

CHAPTER FOUR

HOW TO EDUCATE HIM—
AND ALSO TAKE THE BAR OUT OF
BAR MITZVAH

Your first obligation, as a Jewish parent, is to give your youngster a good Jewish education. The chain of continuity of Jewish history must not be broken. This is obvious; but it is easier said than done. How do you go about fulfilling the Biblical injunction: "And thou shall teach them diligently . . ."?

One way is to transmit the Jewish heritage to your children directly—to educate them at home, to teach them Hebrew, Bible, history, the works. This is ideal, except for one fatal flaw. You yourself may be a big *macher* in the temple and you may have a master's degree in Business Administration, but you are, Jewishly speaking, a functional illiterate, a drop-out, an *"am ha-aretz."* As a boy, you went to a very intense *cheder* (school), but you were wont to slip out the rear window at game time; you dropped out of Hebrew school altogether seven minutes after your own bar mitzvah, breaking the Cleveland record for unilateral withdrawal. You grew up in a home where your immigrant parents spoke a juicy Yiddish, but you, of course, answered in English, thus blowing a chance to learn a language fragrant with the history of your fathers, preferring instead to start up with Latin or German, along with the infinite riches of Beowulf, the Knights of the Round Table, Pocahontas and Frank Merriwell. So how can you teach him? What do you know? What you know are three things, actually: (1) Your child should know what it means to be Jewish;

(2) If you knew, you could tell him; and (3) Since on you they shouldn't count, send him to the temple, let the rabbi worry.

Your child is now enrolled in the Religious School, and you and your wife feel relieved, having disposed of that problem except for the car pool every fourth Sunday. But the very first thing that happens is a special Consecration service at the temple at which your child and thirty others are formally inducted and consecrated, at which the rabbi gives the kids little Torahs and gives you, the parents, a little hell. He preaches a sermon right over the heads of the little ones and drills you right between your eyes, blasting "those among you who have abdicated your own Jewish responsibilities, who push your children out of the car pool and scoot off to the golf course, whose homes are jumping with Chinese art and Polish hams, but who wouldn't know a Jewish book if you tripped over one, whose Jewish ignorance wilts any possible seedling the Religious School might plant in the Negev of the child's mind, whose Jewishness consists of looking for Jewish names in the paper when an airplane crashes, and who have helped to reduce Judaism to a child's plaything, a juvenile Judaism, you have some nerve."

This indictment will shake you up at first, but you will get used to it over the years (the predictable refrain at all parents' meetings, teachers' conferences and Yom Kippur sermons), particularly as you realize that a guilt-edged buckshot charge aimed at everyone really hits no one.

You and your husband rarely go to religious service, except when the rabbi outwits you and announces a "family service," starring thirty performing youngsters from the Religious School, including *guess who*, thus filling up the synagogue like nothing except the High Holy Days, a bazaar or a double bar mitzvah. You go to services as infrequently as you go to the theater—and with about the same I-am-a-critic attitude. You expect a great performance by the rabbi, the cantor, the choir. You are a spectator, sitting on your hands, not a participant in a spiritual occasion of group worship. You and your husband are, as a matter of fact, self-appointed critics—and you mumble your harsh reviews as a blow-by-blow commentary even before the "performance" is over (the cantor is too nasal; the choir too Christian; the rabbi too political—"If he's a preacher, I'm Godzilla"; and the service too cold). Then, later on, when you ask your son to accompany you to temple, you are startled to hear an isolated playback of all your negative reviews to justify his boycott. As our sages say, the rotten apple does not fall far from the tree.

Now your child is on the transmission belt which will educate him Jewishly. He will learn Bible tales, the meaning of the holidays and a little Jewish history. In fact, these are the things he will learn each year. The teachers will change—the subject matter (and even some of the books) will endure. But, after a few years, your Harold will start rebelling. He will sneak out of the bedroom window in the middle of the night, leaving a dummy in his bed. He will run out of the temple and pull a false fire alarm and then disappear up a tree. He will place thumbtacks on the teacher's seat, hoping to be evicted. He will remove the spark plugs of all cars involved in the car pool, not forgetting to cut the telephone wires at each home. He will, in short, become a "disciplinary problem," spending every Sunday morning roaming the halls like a wandering Jew, driving the principal to distraction and the rabbi right up the wall.

The rabbi constantly bemoans the failures of Jewish education in America. He quotes a famous study which concluded that Jewish education in America is "a mile wide and an inch deep." He blames the parents for this failure, pointing out that most parents withdraw their children right after the bar (or bas, for girls) mitzvah: "It is a sin that they do not insist their children go on, at least to Confirmation. They quit just when their minds are mature enough to learn! It is a sin, a tragedy! They turn Jewish education into a juvenile training program—they turn the temple into a bar mitzvah factory. How I wish we could compel each child to stay on, at least through high school." Then his eye falls on you, Harold's parents. "Well, maybe not *every* child! I mean, we don't need overkill either! Some children take to Jewish education like an Al Fatah to Golda Meir! Your Harold, for example, I wouldn't cry if he quit *before* bar mitzvah. He would like that, would he not?"

"Of course *he* would like it," you explain to the rabbi. "That is precisely why he *stays!* Harold may be a weak link, but it won't be *he* who breaks the chain of continuity! We wouldn't give him the satisfaction. He *stays*—at least until bar mitzvah, even if *you* have to put Jewish content into him *intravenously!*"

HOW TO GET THE BAR OUT OF BAR MITZVAH

Well, here you are at a critical moment in the life cycle of your son. He is now approaching his bar mitzvah, the ceremony which marks his thirteenth birthday, and according to tradition, his religious coming of age. The bar mitzvah ceremony is a rite of passage which symbolizes his assumption of responsibility to the congregation and to the Jewish community. It is, potentially, a shaping moment in the development of your son. If you handle this occasion properly, it may help to turn your young man in the direction of genuine values and Jewish purpose.

But you must avoid the pitfalls of letting the religious meaning of the event be eclipsed by the social extravaganzas which sometimes follow the service. At least a year before the big day, talk to your wife. . . .

"Honey, listen. I've been thinking. We've got to start planning the bar mitzvah. Let's make sure that our bar mitzvah doesn't get turned into one of those wild bashes we've attended. . . ."

"I know just what you mean, dear," your wife says. "Like that mod bar mitzvah party on the Island where they had a cage of two hundred parakeets suspended from the ceiling and the cage was opened prematurely, ruining seventy-five pounds of stuffed dherma as well as the chopped liver sculpture of the bar mitzvah boy!"

"Yes, honey," you say. "And remember that other time where they had circus clowns, performing dogs and an elephant bearing the bar mitzvah boy who tried to bow and fell into the punch bowl which had been spiked with gin over the objection of the rabbi, who had fought in vain for a 'modicum of dignity'?"

"Of course," your wife replies. "But that wasn't the worst. Remember that bar mitzvah last year which celebrated the miracle of the Mets? The synagogue social hall was decked out in astroturf and the volunteer choir sang 'The Impossible Dream.' Each boy wore a yarmulka with a Met visor. The cake was baked in the shape of Ron Swoboda belly-flopping across Shea Stadium, and the *zayde* was disguised as Casey Stengel and he went around telling all the kids to eat 'slow but fast.'"

"Oh, yes," you recall, "that was a ball. But what about that African safari in Westchester? The boys dressed up as lions and tigers. Ten body-painted spear carriers seated the guests at numbered tables and served drinks in coconut shells. Remember? The band pounded bongo drums, the lights faded out, and a spotlight picked up the bar mitzvah boy being borne on a litter, like a Middle East potentate, while his weeping grandparents kissed his ring."

"Of course I remember, darling. But what's the point of all this? We're certainly not going to compete with those psychedelic fantasies!"

You should take this opportunity to explain things to your wife. "Look, dear, these unseemly parties indicate what we're up against. We've got to resist the temptation to compete with friends and relatives who think the bar mitzvah is a cross between an off-Broadway production and the coronation of a new pope."

"Of course," she says. "You don't have to tell me that."

"I know, but we have a rare opportunity to convey to Harold our OWN values, to show him that we do not have to keep up with the Cohens, to demonstrate that we will not permit this great religious milestone to be corrupted by status-climbing ostentation. Don't you agree, darling?"

"Of *course*, dear. The last thing I want is all that *show!* So what are you getting at—have I suggested Harold be bar mitzvahed on the Johnny Carson show?"

"No, but let's keep ours simple and fine. After the service, we could have a little kiddush (a prayer over the wine) and a small, informal reception with wine, sponge cake, challah, chopped liver and tea. If we invite just a few close friends and relatives, we can avoid selling our soul to a caterer, and it won't cost us a small fortune and it will have dignity."

"Of course *dignity*, but what do you mean a FEW close friends and relatives? Harold's bar mitzvah doesn't come up every year, you know. It's a once-in-a-lifetime thing. You think I can ignore the girls from the Sisterhood? They all invited us to theirs, you know. Can we insult our neighbors? The people at your office? And how can I draw the line in the family? Are you

going to tell me Aunt Molly is kosher but Uncle Tevya is
trefe? We'll have to invite everybody from the Family Circle;
otherwise, we're bound to antagonize."

"But darling, can't we keep the guest list down low enough
so we won't have to call in a caterer?"

"Not call in a *caterer?*" she cries. "Thank you very much. I
suppose you want *me* to cook and serve for two hundred people?
Am I to spend my own son's bar mitzvah slaving in the kitchen,
so you can get along without a caterer?"

"Sorry, dear, I didn't understand. We'll hire a caterer, of
course, but, please, let's keep it simple and dignified. Let's
have a plain stand-up buffet so . . ."

"STAND UP? Darling, my mother has been waiting for
this moment for thirteen years; she's seventy-two years old and
she has arthritis and you want her to STAND UP? How can
you begrudge me?"

"I'm sorry, honey, I didn't mean that. Standing, sitting—
that's not the point I'm driving at. Let it be a sit-down luncheon.
Let it be catered. Invite the telephone book. But, for heaven's
sake, let's not destroy the religious atmosphere by having the
reception at one of those phony hotels or catering halls
which . . ."

"So where should the reception be? On a boat? In a tent?
On the Merv Griffin show? In the social hall of the temple, I
suppose? Honey, where have you *been* for the past five years?
Don't you know that we now have a building fund to put up a
decent social hall for the temple because the present one is so
small and dingy that it is all right for adult education but
simply NOT ADEQUATE FOR A HIGH-CLASS WED-
DING OR A BAR MITZVAH? Of course, we want the bar
mitzvah to have dignity, but do you have no respect for Harold?
Are we going to ask his friends and relatives to celebrate the
high point of his life in a gloomy room which Cantor Eppes
himself has said reminds him of the waiting room at Garfunkle
Funeral Parlor?"

"Darling, we could decorate it and make it look . . ."

"Like the Bel-Aire Hotel? Exactly! Then why shouldn't we
just go to the Bel-Aire in the first place? Dignity is not *where*
the reception takes place, honey, it's *how* it's *done.* I mean, if

you don't want Harold to have a bar mitzvah, why don't you just say so? Why are you such a party-pooper?"

"Oh, stop it! I'm not pooping anything. Of COURSE I want to see Harold bar mitzvahed, but I just don't want to convert it into another one of those freaky carnivals with strolling accordion players. . . ."

"Tell me, what's so undignified about having one or two nice Jewish accordion players going from table to table? A little joy, a little music, a little *freilichkeit* is no sin, you know."

"Oh, I don't object to accordion players per se, you know that. It's the PRINCIPLE of the thing. And, above all, I want to make sure that Harold shares our values, that he doesn't see the bar mitzvah as a giant giveaway show in which he is cock of the walk, center of the universe, surrounded by people whose function it is to shower him with gifts. He's only thirteen years old, and he's not the *dauphin!* THAT'S WHAT I MEAN!"

"I'm sure he understands that as well as we do, honey. Talk to him."

Now that you have persuaded your wife, it's time for the other shoe to drop. Talk to Harold. Good luck.

"Look, Harold, I'm sure I don't have to say this to you, you're a good kid, but your mommy and I want to make sure that your bar mitzvah is a spiritual experience and not another one of these schmaltzy, overstuffed things where the emphasis is on the BAR and not the MITZVAH. Do you understand?"

"Of course, Dad."

"Then turn off that damn TV and look at me! Your mommy and I know you are a sensitive young man and will co-operate with us in keeping this in good taste and within decent bounds. Okay?"

"Okay, Dad."

"I'm so glad you feel that way, son. Now, one of the biggest offenses in some of these bar mitzvahs is that they are pervaded by an almost pagan presence!"

"Well, what's wrong with presents?"

"No, Harold, not *presents*. *Presence!* Sometimes it's just the wrong *presence*."

"Well, so? We can always exchange them for the *right presents*. What's the problem?"

"No problem, Harold, so long as we don't confuse the ends

and the means. The purpose of the bar mitzvah is to usher you into the Jewish community as a full and responsible member. It is not to collect an assortment of crazy gifts—clothes that won't fit you, books you won't ever read, savings bonds and cash."

"How much cash, Dad? What can I figure?"

"Whaddya mean, how much cash? How do I know? That's exactly the point, Harold, these material things are just not important. In fact, I was thinking that it would be nice to send a note to the people we invite, asking them not to bring gifts. Maybe we could ask them, instead, to give to your favorite charity. What *is* your favorite charity?"

"I am, Dad."

"Don't be corny, Harold. What a lovely, moving thing it would be if we put a moratorium on gifts, telling people we want them to be with us for themselves alone, not their gifts, and that the meaning of the day is religious, not commercial. Dammit, didn't I tell you to turn off the TV? Now what's your reaction, son? How about it, Harold?"

"Dad, let me tell you like it is. I've broken my teeth for a full year, learning my Torah portion. I've taken orders from Cantor Eppes who is an all-time drag. I don't understand one word of it, but I've memorized it so well I can say it in my sleep. My voice is changing and I sound like a baby chimpanzee, but I'm going to chant my Haftorah even if it breaks up the entire congregation. Mommy has written an original speech for me, thanking you and her and the rabbi and everybody else in sight, and I will recite my lines without a cue card. When the service is over, I will be sloppily kissed by a hundred aunts and cousins, most of whom I couldn't name if my life depended on it. Later, there will be a big party at the hotel with a couple of hundred adults dancing and drinking themselves into the small hours of the morning, none of them even noticing that my friends and I slipped home hours ago to watch the Met game on television. After all that, you want me to take a vow of poverty? My answer, Dad, is simple and non-negotiable: No presents, no Bar Mitzvah!"

And so, predictably, Harold's bar mitzvah reception takes place in the Crystal Room of the Bel-Aire Hotel and is catered by Mama Loshen and the Daughters of the Perpetual

Simcha! The strolling accordionists (Jewish) and all the guests, even including those who are exiled to table 37 behind the second piano, agree that "Thank heaven, this was one bar mitzvah that was done with dignity and in good taste!"

CHAPTER FIVE

HOW TO UNDERSTAND YOUTH VALUES
(INCLUDING THE YICHUS RATING SCALE)

It is important to understand youth people. They are a very special species. It takes one to know one. The author not only WAS one (a juvenile delinquent at twelve), but is surrounded by youth people of his very own (four of them, without whose help this book would have been completed many months earlier). Close contact with this youth generation has convinced me they are indescribable. I shall now describe them.

(1) They are anti-materialistic. They are in revolt against the worship of the bitch goddess money. If THEY do not worship THINGS, the reason is they also reject worship. They are sick and tired of private selfishness masquerading as free enterprise. These young people merely require a car, a beach club, a good hi-fi, an allowance, a cassette tape recorder, a color television, six credit cards, an Arab nargile, sports equipment, two radios and a room of their own with a Princess telephone. They are consumers *extraordinaire*. The anti-materialist conviction is in direct proportion to the distance from poverty. The young people from Beverly Hills and Roslyn Heights are the angriest enemies of affluence. ("How can you send me to college for $4500 a year when the per capita income of the Appalachians is $3000 a year?") Altogether, this generation of young people is the most materialistic anti-materialist generation in American history. Affluence to them is a fat cow, to be alternately kicked and milked. Some of them have burned their draft cards as a symbol of a war they despise. None has yet

burned his Mustang as a symbol of the capitalism they condemn. So, if you are comfortable, prepare yourself to be melted
by the laser beam of their righteousness. If you are poor, you
can try to join the youth people in putting down material
values, but they will hold you in secret contempt for not *making* it. In both cases you lose. Which is, of course, the special
genius of youth who know how to be a pain in the neck and
loved.

(2) They are unselfish. Youth people have had it with
money-making, preoccupation with savings and pensions, buying
financial security in the father's business or a large corporation.
They are the first generation with a vision which transcends the
circle of the family. They share everything with their peers, a
gentle world-wide community of youth. As it was with the Jews
in all ages, there is among the youth a vast, informal, un-
structured network all across the world where anyone can get
food, transportation, or lodging—an "underground railroad,"
with local stops at every campus, for members of the youth
tribe.

Young people are concerned with the problems of the entire
society, especially the poor and the black. They recoil from
being programmed by our technocratic society. They feel that
they have been manipulated. Their solution? To manipulate
others—their schools, their universities and (especially) their
parents. The object of their unselfishness is to achieve spontaneity, freedom and happiness (for themselves). They are
beautiful, but they are the most self-centered unselfish generation yet. If you suggest sharing their allowances with the
starving peons of Bolivia, what do you think they will say?
Right on!

(3) They are deeply opposed to racism. This causes a certain amount of ambivalence and confusion. When black extremists demand separatism and denounce white liberals as
honkies, white youth must shift gears quickly. Instead of being
against all racism, black and white, they must zero in on white
racism. After all, didn't the Kerner Commission come out
against "white racism" and isn't that doubly impressive because the report was written by white racists? Okay, but how
will youth people know a "white racist" when they see one?
Easy. In the first place, he is white. Beyond that, it is not

necessary for him to either hold racist views or practice racial discrimination. It is enough for him to be associated with "institutional racism" which can be measured by the WHITE RACIST PIG QUOTIENT. Is the person a policeman, a teacher, a clergyman, a politician, a businessman, a social worker, a public official? Is he over thirty-five? Is he married to a white mate, thus perpetuating racial segregation in his home, the crucible of racist values? Does he live in a white neighborhood? Has he ever referred to a virtuous person as "pure as the driven snow?" Why doesn't he blue-list people from the club—why *black*-list? Has he referred to a bad scene as a *"black* day?" Why not *mauve* for mourning instead of black? Does he lament *finster mazel* (black luck)? Does he tell "white lies"? Has he protested calling the presidential mansion the White House. Does he fancy God is white and male, compounding chauvinisms? It is, clearly, easy to identify white racist piggery, especially in you who, let's face it, never lived in Harlem or learned Swahili or visited Africa, wouldn't know a hominy grit from a halvah and, *mirabile dictu*, live in a white house in the suburbs.

Most Jewish youngsters get a great deal out of college. For one thing, they discover real live Negroes to be liberal with, which is more than they had when they were liberal in their nice homogenized white suburbs. For many Jewish youngsters, contact with real blacks was like revelation. Some made a religion out of blackness. They worshiped at the altar of black power. They made a noble ritual out of exorcising white racism. Some anointed the late Malcolm X, Eldridge Cleaver, Stokely Carmichael and James Forman. But much of it's gone sour.

The handwriting was on the wall when black students disrupted a small liberal arts college in Iowa. The non-negotiable demand was simple and blunt: black studies. But, knowing full well that their white allies from Scarsdale would otherwise beat them to the building, the black rebels dispatched their fleetest track stars to hotfoot it across the campus and take over the building first and bolt the doors. The white radicals, wearing "Honkies for Huey" buttons, milled around on the outside, sheepishly, sending in food parcels and hand-scribbled notes, like "We are with you. But you don't want to be with *us*. We understand perfectly. Why should you want to be with us honkies? You are right to despise us. We despise *ourselves*. And why should you want the assistance of anybody who despises himself? You don't have to answer this. We understand. Up against the wall with honkies like us! Up the Revolution!"

A few of the white youths then began to understand what the black revolution on campus was all about. It wasn't—as black rhetoric pretended—that the university was a "white racist institution." (The more liberal the college, the more it was condemned as racist.) It wasn't ROTC or Dow Chemical or that jazz. It wasn't that blacks couldn't get into the university; on the contrary, the Administration had no less than seven posses roaming the ghettos and kidnaping kicking black youngsters into the SEEK program, not to mention the bounty for black Ph.D's to teach black studies. The real truth was NOT that integration had failed. The truth was that it had SUCCEEDED too *well*. The black collegians had been worn out by integration. Every white liberal had to have a black student with whom to walk to class, eat, and be seen at the library. Every white girl had to have a black boy to date. You couldn't blame the whites. They had been raised on a diet of racial liberalism in an apartheid community; now, for the first time, there were real blacks through whom to fulfill that abstract liberalism and sublimate the years of hypocrisy. But you couldn't blame the blacks either. They got exhausted. There were simply not enough blacks to provide an ornament—a human mezuzah or St. Christopher's medal—for every white student. So the blacks decided, the hell with this noise! Separatism may be kooky in theory but, dammit, it's a hell of a lot easier on the nerves in practice.

So the blacks decided to "get themselves together" and go for black studies. Egged on by a handful of black professors in gray-flannel dashikis, the university administration, leaking guilt to starboard because they recognized that blacks had been effectively blacked out (sic) of American history, surrendered before they saw the whites of the black eyes. But did that solve the problem? No. Everybody knew that the moment black studies were established, the class would fill up with white satellites, and black students wouldn't be able to get in without a shoehorn. So, inevitably, the black students had to shift their nonnegotiable demand: SEPARATE AND AUTONOMOUS BLACK STUDIES; SEPARATE BLACK DORMITORIES.

By this time, it dawned on more of the white students that maybe they weren't wanted.

Many Jewish youngsters were hard hit by this rejection. But the wisest among them understood it. Why shouldn't blacks be left alone to define their own identity, to find out *who* and *what* they are? Indeed, a few Jewish college students stopped to reflect; if *they* must find out what *their* identity is, what about *my* identity? What does my Jewishness mean to *me*? A thousand Jewish college students at Cornell petitioned for Jewish studies on the campus. And a group of Jewish students drew up a list of non-negotiable demands for "Jewish power" (see Chapter Eight).

All this has caused some strain in black-Jewish relationships on the college campus. The best means of reconciliation is to pump more *black Jews* into the colleges. One black Jew, an aficionado of Hebrew and Talmud, was among the leading black rebels who occupied the communications building at one of our New England universities. He issued a series of tough-sounding, fire-and-brimstone communiques from the building newly renamed Malcolm X University. But, at the height of the confrontation, the lad's *zoftig* black Jewish mother appeared on the scene, stood outside the building with her hands on her hips and shouted, "Sammy, THIS IS YOUR MOTHER! YOU GOT TEN SECONDS TO GET YOUR BLACK TOCHAS OUT OF THERE OR I'LL BREAK YOUR YIDDISH KOP!" Sammy popped out of that building like he was propelled from Cape Kennedy. Black power is formidable, indeed, but it cannot withstand a Jewish mother, black or white.

(4)   A few (less than 1 per cent) are revolutionaries on the cheap. These Kwatch-Marxist Jacobins denounce our entire system as corrupt and fascist. They spin romantic fantasies about Che and Eldridge Cleaver, Ho and Mao Tse Tung. Their manifestoes are as revolutionary and wild-eyed as the proclamations of the Red Guard. Ernest Van den Haag, author of *The Jewish Mystique*, describes "revolutionary activity as the Jewish equivalent of juvenile delinquency." But, before you call in J. Edgar Hoover or cut your little one out of your will (you may have to do that later in Chapter Seven), realize that their statements are like cactus—prickly and threatening on the outside, soft and mushy on the inside, an ideological mishmash of

Cleaver and the Beatles. You've got to strip away the flaming polemics like so many layers of onionskin. And, after you've done that, what do they really want, these flame-throwing revolutionaries? Better dormitory rules. A larger allowance. The right to pass out literature. A youth lounge. No parietals. Swahili. Black studies. Legalize marijuana. Ban Saran Wrap. The actual demands are the biggest anti-climax of the Revolution. So don't let them scare you out of your wits.

(5) They want a new code of sexual freedom. They reject our concept that sex is sinful outside of marriage. They see nothing wrong with premarital sex and they believe that our adult world is all hung up in sexual hypocrisy. They are right about us of course. The advent of the pill has transformed sexual relations and the young recognize that. But the real danger is not that they will destroy the Puritan code of sexual morality; we did that a long time ago. The real problem is that, far from escalating sex, these young people take it for granted like pizza, rock, and desert boots. When we were in high school and college, we thought of only one thing. Sex dominated our consciousness. When we weren't lying about it, we were fantasying about it or inventing adventures for the titillation of our friends. Our young ones don't even talk about it. It is just another part of the scenery. Besides, the difference between girls and boys has been all but obliterated. We can forgive them for throwing our schools into turmoil, challenging our political system, and crucifying a thousand college presidents, but we can never forgive them for demythologizing sex! The colleges haven't helped—if sex were against the rules, there would be a lot more of it around. Under youth hegemony, sex has gone to pot, and boys and girls treat each other like brothers and sisters in a gigantic mishpocha. Sex in America is becoming a spectator sport, there is more of it in the movies than in the balconies, and the young have helped wreck it. Shame on them! Sex is dead!

And now, to complicate matters further, thousands of girls are organizing Women's Liberation Fronts to combat male chauvinism and to "end sexual exploitation of females in our society." These chicks will probably end up throwing out the baby (if we can still produce such a thing) with the bath. They are picketing Playboy clubs, demanding the erection of separate (but equal) Playboy clubs where handsome young men will serve drinks to girl customers, announcing: "I'm David, your bull!" Some of these girls are forswearing sex altogether because they claim their bodies are exploited. If Attorney General John (and Martha) Mitchell can get rid of the "liberal Communists" in our midst, they should be able to put an end to this anti-American campaign by broad-minded broads like this who burn their bras and are about to screw up our vital élan!

(6) They believe in participatory democracy. Each person must do his own thing, power to the people. They want the voting age reduced to eighteen because they have the right to participate in decisions which affect their future, right? But if we give them the vote, will they use it? Not on your life! Vote —for what? Don't you know that Nixon and Humphrey are the same creature? When are you going to reject this "lesser of two evils" tyranny and realize that in the end it is still evil? The pure method is to regard the political process as contaminated, the voting booth as a chamber of horrors and all candidates as objects of scorn. Besides, the politicians are pawns, if not queens, and why dignify them with our attention? Thus, the real job of youth is rhetorical, which is a hell of a lot easier than working. After you've cut through the rhetoric, you will find—zounds!—that most young people are sitting on their duffs just like the older generation they condemn. The young have discovered the oldest cop out in human experience!

(7) The young believe in spontaneity. They are sick of being the passive receiving sets TV turned them into. The activists among them can spend six weeks planning a spontaneous demonstration. The important thing is honesty . . . tell it like it is. Every youth his own foolproof, shockproof crap-detector. Relationships should be loving and tender. One shouldn't conceal feelings—positive and negative. Touch a lot. But don't spare people either. If a boy takes out a blind date and finds she looks like a fire hydrant, he doesn't try to figure out a soft deceit to get her home without hurt feelings. He stands at the door next to her father and says, "Cheez, baldy, your chick's a beast! She's as ugly as Mayor Daley—and twice as fat! Good-by, Columbus!" Everybody respects such honesty, brutal as it is. Enough with the deceptions and hypocrisy of the

good people. What the world needs in this phony civilized era is some good, clean cannibalism in human relations. If God is dead, can't youth people resurrect the Lord of the Flies?

(8) They are anti-semantic. Jews are the People of the Book, but our children haven't even read the minutes of the last meeting, much less the *Pirke Avot* (The Sayings of the Fathers). One of the social diseases of American life is verbal diarrhea. Our children have been raised by babbling TV sets acting as baby sitters. This is the first generation of Americans to come home from the hospital nursery to find a color TV waiting in the crib. Words, speeches, rhetoric have poured over our children like a flood. They feel drowned in words. So they have become anti-semantic. Rhetoric bores them. The only sermon they respect is the deed. And they judge us not by what we say, or what we say we believe, but by what we do. This is cruel, and if we did the same to them, we'd reduce them to impotence, for some of them have substituted polemics for politics, despair for reason, and frank talk for sex. So, who is more alienated, we or they? Who is more Jewish, we or they?

Not knowing who or what to believe, I conducted my own survey of the Jewish attitudes of eighty-seven Jewish young persons. Some 58 per cent said: "Tell me, what do you mean by JEWISH?" Approximately 11.3 per cent said: "I'm part of the silent majority and I'm not going to break silence for your mishuganer survey!" Some 9.1 per cent said I was invading their privacies. Approximately 4.6 per cent cried: "Police brutality!" Some 2.7 per cent said: "What do you want from me? I didn't choose to be born Jewish." One angry young rebel refused to talk because his Jewish parents had cut off his credit at the pizza parlor. Another bearded rebel said: "How could *my* father have worn a beard? *His* father had a beard!" Two youngsters invoked the fifth (Commandment). One sang: "Radishes are red: the sky is bluish; when I'm in love, the whole world's Jewish." Another: "*Look* says we'll vanish, *Life* says we'll die— we'll no doubt survive them both—but, just in case, Columbus, good-by!"

This survey, albeit limited in its sample, nonetheless illuminates some of the ambiguities, ambivalences and hubris of contemporary American Jewish life. It indicates, does it not, that the situation is hopeless but not serious? Remember that an optimist says this is the best of all possible worlds; a pessimist *agrees.*

(9)   The young have had it with deferred gratifications. They are sick of the race to Harvard which begins at the age of three with the frenzied competition to get into a good nursery school, being driven to earn good grades from early childhood to get into a good college, to engage in fierce competition in order to prepare for a good career in the rat race, to spend a life moving up the pecking order, to save for the future. What future? Many American kids don't believe they'll be alive in ten years. And who wants to be programmed for life, plugged into a computerized machine, in the vague hope of enjoying long-deferred satisfactions in some distant future while the world trembles on the Gillette-edge of nuclear disaster? So they are a NOW generation, and they talk from the belly of the whale! For many Jewish youngsters, this means unconsciously plunging into the past, not the future. Instead of living in Roslyn Heights and Highland Park, which their parents reached after slaving in backbreaking upward mobility, the youngsters opt for downward mobility, retracing old family roots to live in the pad on Houston Street on the Lower East Side, the Hill District of St. Paul, and the ghettos of America's cities, which their grandparents occupied and fled a generation ago. And what do they want most to do? Become wandering Jews, hitchhiking over the face of the earth to countries their forefathers fled. Live on a farm with an outhouse as their impoverished immigrant grandparents did in Tamaqua, Pennsylvania, sixty years ago when they came to the Golden Medinah from Pinsk, Russia! Thus does the *now* generation become the THEN generation; thus does the third generation revert to the way of life of the first generation, wiping out your generation in the process; go fight City Hall.

(10)   They are not afraid of drugs. As we pop pep pills into our mouth to get through the day and belt a cocktail at lunch and another before dinner and half a bottle before facing people we dislike, many of them see nothing wrong with smoking a joint of marijuana. This drives us wild. It is against the law, we cry—we Americans who drive over the speed limit, cut corners on our income tax, litter the streets, jaywalk, and shlepp our fifteen-year-old children into the moviehouse for half price

by having them walk on their knees. Yes, it is bad for their
health, we insist, and it may well be, but not nearly so bad
as cigarette smoking which makes our insides look like the
black hole of Oh, Calcutta. Aha, we say, almost everybody who
goes on to hard drugs starts with marijuana, which may be
true but as logical as saying they also began with milk. So the
drug scene spreads among the young (not to mention lawyers,
doctors, clergymen and other Establishment types unmolested
by the cops) while adults demand busts, law and order and
campus espionage, all of which merely intensify the youth determination to defy us, reinforcing their conviction that we
adults are childish Chelmites. If we legalized pot, it would be
efficiently administered by the Mafia, advertised on "The Tonight Show," and sold in machines at the neighborhood drug-
store, and the young would soon get as bored with it as they are
with dirty movies. They might, in their ennui, rediscover sex.

(11) They reject superficialities. They go for the essence,
like the jugular vein. So do not fret about their appearance—
clothes, hair, feet, etc. They will prefer moldy World War II
clothes and shoes hammered out of bald tires—these are their
identification cards. The boys will use their faces as launching
pads for zapata mustaches, ponytails, and Hari-Krishna smiles.
These are their ways of saying No to the conventions of neat-
ness, conformity, and respectability. (Any real non-conformist
among them would get a crew cut, but this is quibbling.) Do
not get uptight about beards. If a beard was okay for Abraham,
Moses, Aristotle, Plato and Joe Namath, why must you kvetch?
And the Bible socks it to you: "Ye shall not round the corners
of your heads, neither shalt thou mar the corners of thy beard"
(Leviticus). So what's with all your thou-shalt-nots?

How should you, the parent, react when Harold returns from
hitchhiking across the country, like a thumbing Bedouin, looking like an Australian bushman? What should you say when
your Beth drops in at a Family Circle meeting wearing a maxi-
shmotte and grandma spectacles and with her bare feet so caked
with tar and sand from the beach that the footprints leave a
psychedelic pattern on your Namath-type white llama rug, turning it into a throw-rug Rorschach test? Don't just sit there,
acquiescent and helpless like some parental cretin. Assert yourself. Maintain your standards. Say things like: "This is just a

stage" and "I don't care what you do *elsewhere*, but in this house you will obey US!" And: "I don't care how long you let your hair grow, but at least stop tripping over it and put it in pigtails, Melvin!" Or: "You have an entire wardrobe upstairs and you run around wearing shmottes, Hush Puppies and peace buttons. At least let me give your clothes to the Salvation Army!" Or: "Mother and I don't care about appearances, you know that, and if you don't get that burning bush defoliated by tonight at 6:00 P.M., we're going to slash our wrists!"

One seventeen-year-old hippie, hitchhiking across the country, was picked up in Wyoming (hitchhiking is illegal in Wyoming) by a red-necked sheriff, who gets a bounty for every hippie from the East. The boy was placed in a cell for three days with adult criminals, and had his burning bush shaved by the sadistic guardians of the public weal. (These harsh minions of the law may bring about the ultimate generation gap: parents on one side of the bars, the kids on the other.) The young Samson was incensed and humiliated. But, like the Biblical Samson, he was also weakened. Shorn of his locks, he could no longer function. Standing on the side of the road with his head glistening in the sun, blinding several of the passing motorists, he was avoided by his own passing hirsute trible, but he was also rejected by the straights who took him for an army deserter. If you're interested, you will find Samson, thumb frozen from the Wyoming winter, standing on the road at Laramie, disguised as a Burma Shave sign. It's a hair-raising experience, but remember there is no such thing as *hippies*—there is only an individual *kid* with plenty of troubles of which you may be one.

(12) One reason communication between the young and us is so bad is because we adults do not HEAR them. This isn't because of any generation gap or differing perspectives, or even because they say "bullshit" to everything we say. It's because, in one short Chanukah vacation, their souped-up stereo record player at full blast will blow out your eardrums. From then on, communication will improve. You'll hear nothing but static which will come mostly from your livid neighbors. In raising kids, better deaf than dumb. Thank your lucky stars for the generation gap. You would rather have teen-age buddies, calling you by your first name?

(13) They are not afraid. Sam Levenson, the schoolteacher

turned comedian, once described American education as a hierarchy built on fear: "Teachers are afraid of the principal. The principal is afraid of the supervisor. The supervisor is afraid of the superintendent. The superintendent is afraid of the school board. The school board is afraid of the mayor. The mayor is afraid of the parents. The parents are afraid of their children. And the children, God bless them, aren't afraid of anybody!" Amen.

(14) They are religious. Whether experimenting in astrology, mysticism, witchcraft, rock, pot, scientology, vegetarianism, omphaloskepsis or philosophy, many young people are in search —of faith, purpose, meaning, belief, ultimate truth. They are thrashing about, sometimes childishly, for ideals to hold on to in a chaotic world. They are yearning for the absolute, the sacred and the ecstatic. In short, they are in a *religious* quest, and thus they naturally reject our churches and synagogues, our building funds and membership drives, our superrationality, our edifice complexes and Mickey Mouse projects and our "bazaar religion." We cannot forgive them their rejection, but it might be helpful to remember the ancient Midrash in which God himself is quoted as saying about His people, and I quote: "Would that they forgot *Me* and remembered My Commandments." A lesser deity, Harvey Cox, refers to a "new monasticism" in which the young participate with "vows of poverty, obedience to a life-style and a kind of chastity that prevents sex from creating divisions in the community."

(15) In understanding their values, bear in mind that they are acting out your fantasies. Would you really be happier if your child was a vitamin? And, also, remember this: youth is a social disease which, like acne, time alone will cure. It happens 100 times out of 100!

THE YICHUS RATING SCALE (YRS)

Today's youth generation—especially the campus generation —has a scale of values all its own. It is a complete reversal of the traditional Protestant ethic as well as the standards of piety and scholarship venerated by Jewish tradition. Do you want to know where you stand on such a scale? If so, you're a masochist. If not, you are curious yellow.

If your forebears came over on the Mayflower, you are a fink, which automatically costs you five points and makes you personally responsible for enslaving the blacks, massacring the Indians, polluting and setting fire to Lake Erie, persecuting the Jews, and electing Nixon.

If you (or your spouse) have built up a good business and saved up a little money by dint of thrift and sacrifice, you are a "capitalist moneygrubber" and that will cost you four points.

If you live in suburbia, it doesn't do any good if you do not drink, have never danced the Dayenu Cha Cha Cha at the Sodom and Gomorrah Country Club, or if you have knocked yourself out to integrate the community and to help the poor. You are a "fat suburbanite" (even if you're so thin that when your children give you the needle, it comes out the other side), which is as reprehensible to the young today as being an "integrationist" in the fifties was to the local crackers in the South. This not only costs you three points. It disqualifies you from having an opinion on the urban crisis, because (even if you were BORN in the suburb) you have "no right to talk about the city, seeing how you middle-class racist whites deserted the city, running away from the blacks, and are therefore responsible for the entire mess."

If you express enthusiasm for any political candidate, you reveal yourself as both a square and a social fascist. You must realize that your candidate and his opponent are Tweedledee and Tweedledum and both are equally irrelevant. By definition, no truly good man can be designated by our political processes which are rotten to the core. It's like Groucho Marx who said he wouldn't join any country club that would have him as a member. If you prefer your candidate because he is more "liberal" than the other, your deficit soars from 2 to 3 because a liberal, as you should certainly know by now, is a neuter gender, lacking both brains and balls. If you indulge your folly to the point of actually going out and *voting* for your man, your minus sinks to 4 and you deserve the blame you will get. If, on the other hand, you adopt the purism of your youngsters, you too can spend the rest of your life in lofty superiority, muttering "no choice, no vote" while the whole society goes down the drain.

If your wife has a black maid, you get an automatic —1 for

"exploitation" whether you call her Sue, Miss Sue or Miss Stargell, whether you underpay or overpay (in your house, you'll *overpay*) and whether she is happy with you or not. If your help is Scandinavian, French, Italian, or German, this is not "exploitation," it is people-to-people understanding, like having a foreign student in your house for a year.

At the same time, if there are blacks working in your factory (and one black executive, of the Sidney Poitier type, in the window as a symbol of racial opportunity), you are "a genocidal, racist exploiter." If there are no blacks in the shop or in the window, you are "a Georgia-cracker segregationist." You get —3 for saying "colored," —2 for "Negro," but +1 for "Afro-American." The fact that your son wouldn't be caught dead in his father's place (even during summer vacation) does not absolve you from getting with it. Don't oversimplify.

If you sign a blank check for the youth people, defend every cockamamy thing they do, and tell everybody (including the kids) that you are "with them all the way," you lose one full point of credit for "patronizing," which is a major No-No, and you lose two if you call the kids "kids."

But there are also ways to pick up credits, so don't be discouraged:

If you ever spent time in jail in the integration or peace struggle, you get three plus points (but you get two no matter WHAT you served time in jail for, including forgery).

If you were personally denounced by Joe McCarthy or Spiro Agnew, you hit the top of the yichus scale—and you get 10 points (unless, of course, you co-operated by naming names, in which case, move out of the house because the tyrant McCarthy was a pussycat compared to today's young when their sense of rectitude is violated). "My dad was smeared by old Joe McCarthy," is the ultimate yichus and stirs envy and mystery in the hearts of the student's fascinated friends, especially WASPs, whose parents loved Joe and thought Gene unclean.

If you (or your parents) came from the ghetto—either of Eastern Europe or of the cities of the United States—you are a colorful and interesting person, worthy of a 4-point credit. If you had *stayed* in the ghetto, you would be worth at least 10 points today, but that's water over the damn you no longer give. And you certainly rate higher than WASPs who go back to the Mayflower, descend from the Founding Fathers (who are dismissed as "slave-hungry plutocrats"), and who grew up on Beacon Hill or on a corny farm in Iowa.

So now you are ready to take the test:

1. You have a nice business that you spent your life slaving to develop? —2
2. You have a lovely split-level white house in the suburb? —3
3. You have two cars? +1 (This is contradictory but, even if we do not know where we are going in life, you can't get there without transportation, and consistency is the hobgoblin of small minds.)
4. You have two TV sets (one color)? +1. (Man does not live by cars alone.)
5. You give to the NAACP, CORE, and the Urban League? +3
6. You are active in civil rights work? +3
7. You worked for Gene McCarthy or Bobby Kennedy in '68 and John Lindsay in '69? +4
8. You were called up by Joe McCarthy in the 50s? +10, unless you got down on your knees.
9. You have attended a rock festival and, in fact, almost got stomped to death at Woodstock and/or tear gassed at the Moratorium in Washington? +7
10. You once went to jail with Martin Luther King for a demonstration in Alabama? +6
11. You were a wobbly in the 30s? +7
12. You read *Ramparts*, the *Village East Other*, the *New York Review of Books*, *Avant-Garde*, *Screw*, and the *Berkeley Barb*? +4
13. You read *Commentary*, the New York *Post*, *New Republic*, *Nation*, *Midstream*, *Life*, and the *National Jewish Post*? —2
14. You have voted for Cleaver, Gregory, Mailer, or Breslin? +2
15. You don't vote at all as an act of protest against the assorted crumbs and flakes coughed up by our irrelevant political system? +4
16. You were wounded in the Spanish Civil War (unless

you fought for Franco), or the Chicago Democratic Convention? +8

17. You've been maced? +11
18. You haven't eaten a grape in five years? +7
19. You have subpoena envy? +8
20. You put down Pat Moynihan +6, Hayakawa +4, Martha Mitchell +7, and Julius Hoffman +10.
21. You have beaucoup Satyagraha (soul force)? +9
22. You are fully aware of the irrelevance of everything, including yourself, and most especially this ridiculous Yichus Rating Scale? +10

Add it up and it spells disaster, but it at least shows you what you are up against, which is, of course, the wall!

CHAPTER SIX

HOW TO HAVE YOUR HEAD SHRUNK
BEFORE YOUR CHILD PUTS YOU UP
AGAINST THE WALL, MOTHER

It is by now crystal clear that your house is not big enough for both you and your son, Harold. Indeed, it isn't a mere generation gap. It is a wadi so deep that one of you is sure to push the other over the brink. So one of you must be crazy.

Since *you* have been able to get along all these years, despite everything, you must be functioning with reasonable efficiency. There must be something wrong with Harold. As you can tell by reading current literature, what is wrong with Harold is obviously you, his mother.

As for your *husband,* no matter how authoritarian, inept, gracious, gauche, constipated, idealistic or materialistic, he is off the hook. Don't try to put the monkey on *his* back. He will have become invisible by the time Harold hits the psychiatrist couch. Who ever talks about the modern Jewish patriach? Not even the modern Jewish *matriarch!* Does Roth even write a short story about him? Even if the father is magnificent, in our modern society it is the Jewish mother (of all faiths and races) who holds the patent and the reins. After all, when Theodor Herzl was your husband's age, he had already been dead for five years! Therefore, many fathers, seeing the handwriting on the wall, are also becoming Jewish mothers. As Harold grows from adolescence to adultery, it is you, the Jewish mother, who will be blamed for all of Harold's *narishkeit* (hang-ups). So, prepare yourself in advance. See a shrink already!

H2S (Having Head Shrunk) is not an exclusively Jewish game. You don't have to be Jewish to have your head shrunk. Yet it would be foolish to deny that there is a Jewish component to psychology. Not only was Freud, the Big Daddy of psychoanalysis, a Jew; so were most of his disciples and his patients. Although statistics are hard to come by, it seems certain that a high proportion of analysts and patients today are Jews. Their wives are another story; 64 per cent of the Jewish psychiatrists in New Haven have Gentile wives, which means the shrinks are still hung up about *their* Jewish mothers! Does this demonstrate that Jews are more neurotic or merely more sophisticated as to the vagaries of the human mind and emotions?

Maybe both, for indeed Jews are a shrinking percentage in American life, inasmuch as our birth rate is low due to too much time spent at meetings and on the shrink's couch.

I have come to this conclusion as a result of an intensive study among my Jewish friends (all of whom are jointly suing me for invasion of privacy), which demonstrated that if a person is Jewish, had parents, lives in or near a big city, prides himself on being intellectual and swings a bit, then the probabilities of that person being involved in psychological therapy at some point of his life falls in the median range of 70 to 80 per cent. (My friends *do* tend to skew up the normal bell-bottom curve very badly, but this has been discounted in advance.) Why is this? The Jewish answer is: why not?

After all, Jews have been fascinated by the vagaries of the mind since Biblical times. The madness of Saul, the sibling rivalry of Jacob and Esau, the inner anguish of Job, the ethnocentrism of Jonah, the masochism of Jeremiah, the sexual brinkmanship of David, the emotional disabilities of Moses as reflected in his stuttering—the Bible brims with case histories of flesh-and-blood human beings caught up in the web of those basic human emotions we have learned to categorize only within the last century. Jews have always taken their heroes straight, with all their physical and emotional weaknesses. David, Abraham, Moses, Solomon, Saul, Jacob—these are not denatured, pasteurized, pallid wraiths. They are men of warm blood, deep feeling, inner conflicts and great yearning. They are human; they are honorable menschen! They all may have been touched by the hand of God, but even that made them more—not *less*—human. They argued with Him, challenged Him, defied Him; they stormed and raged and anguished; there was not a plastic saint among them. They seethed with life, and this is why the Bible has been a living document to our very day. To help keep man human, especially in an age of increasing dehumanization, is perhaps the central meaning of the Jewish way of life.

And what was true in the days of the Bible has been the enduring motif of the Jewish people for three thousand years —an intoxication with life (*L'chaim*) and an illogical belief (against impossible odds) that man is good and the world can be improved. There is no room in the Jewish tradition for quiet-ism, for passing the buck to God to correct the wrongs of human existence, for ascetic denial of the sexual and other basic emotional drives, for otherworldly retreat to the artificial peace of monastery and convent. Catholic priests are now trying to shuck off celibacy; shucks, Jews sanctified sexuality three thousand years ago. Judaism is a passionate encounter with life, and the encounter lies in the arena of action in this world. In such a value system, the pursuit of physical and emotional health can only be regarded as blessed. Jews, therefore, took to the adventure of inner space—the exploration of the mind and the emotions—with the excitement with which the world at large responds to the heart-stopping drama of outer space.

Besides, many of my friends are nutty as fruitcakes, spending their time with the friendly neighborhood shrink.

DECIDING ON H2S

The following are acceptable reasons for you to decide on H2S:
1. Everybody else is doing it.
2. Harold has raised a query as to the relevancy of parents.
3. You are the kind of person who, when you are telling a story and it is momentarily interrupted (say, for example, when the three-year-old son of the hostess suddenly bursts into the room and damply demands: "All right, who is the wise guy who left the toilet seat up?"), nobody, but nobody, ever asks you to *finish* your story.
4. You write Herzoglike letters to U Thant, Nasser and

Arthur Goldberg, which you never mail, yet you are furious they do not reply.

5. You can't stand Harold's hair before breakfast.
6. You have a bad case of the blahs because of your role as mother earth.
7. You have never learned how to tell your own telephone-prone mother: "Listen, I'm putting you on *hold!*"
8. The shrink, like the rabbi, doesn't make house calls.
9. Because you enjoy good conversation, you talk only to yourself.
10. You are afraid of loud noises, of which Harold is the most frightening.
11. Harold has accused you of nudging, castrating, seducing, tyrannizing, bowdlerizing and ignoring him—in short, he is driving you mishugah, and can Little Red Riding Hood handle the wolf?

PICKING THE HEADSHRINKER

This is the moment of truth. Do you select a psychiatric analyst, a lady analyst, a non-analytic psychiatrist, a directive psychologist, a phrenologist, a Jungian, an Alderian, a Freudian? Take the guy nearest your home; traffic is terrible and trying to park in the city would make a nervous wreck out of you.

Within two years you will face the choice again because you will be fed up with your doctor and tired of hearing about *his* problems—especially his *kid* who is chief of the crazies at the University of Michigan and goes around burning up deans on "The Today Show." In changing, be sure that 1) your new doctor is more expensive than the first, thus showing your friends you are not regressing; 2) your new doctor will accept transfer credits for your past work; 3) your new doctor is of the opposite sex (from you, I mean), because by now you know something of the tricky mechanism of transference and will feel more comfortable being in love with a doctor of the opposite sex; 4) this doctor is the one your friend has been "working with" for twelve years (as your friend puts it, "He's not *good*, but he's *stable*"); 5) you can buy hot bagels nearby and there is ample parking within a block of his office so that you will not come to the sessions late, sweating, and hostile. Don't minimize this.

One of my friends spent seven lean years getting his head shrunk in Manhattan and, when he was all cured, he had to spend two years in jail (where his head swelled up again) as a scofflaw for the parking tickets accumulated while he was on the couch. Was it worth it? (When the wan patient after the long years in the clink put this question to the doctor, the doctor replied typically: "Well, what do YOU think?" and the patient gave him a non-directive belt to the kop which provoked the doctor to exclaim: "Now, *why* did you do *that?* YOU ARE A DAMN RECIDIVIST!"

THE FIFTY-MINUTE HOUR

First of all, why fifty minutes?!! If he charges by the HOUR what's this 50 MINUTE jazz? Get this off your chest right away. It will consume the first five sessions but it will clear the air. Thereafter, to derive maximum benefit from therapy, observe the following rules:

1. Figure out if he is Jewish. For God's sake, don't come out and ASK him because that will be counterproductive and time-consuming. (If he knows Al Capp is Jewish and he [the doctor] regrets it, he's *Jewish*.)
2. Don't make it easy for him to find out if YOU are Jewish.
3. Lie down, rest a little. That bumper-to-bumper traffic can kill you.
4. Tell him the latest psychiatrist joke.
5. Compel him to give you a yes or no answer to *something*.
6. Explain to him that you do not want to continue to talk to yourself all the time because you are becoming a bore.
7. Make him show emotion (bring a cobra, or arrive in the office stark naked, or bring your pornograph to talk to his pornograph, or pour hot tea on him). Don't just lie there passively as if he is a television set, or he won't respect you and will stop listening after the third session at the very latest.

Remember, headshrinking is show biz!

RESULT OF H2S

By now you should have been freed of your emotional hang-ups and of $13,787. When you are interrupted in the middle of a story, you now will have the strength to stand up and roar: AS I WAS SAYING, DAMMIT . . . You will no longer be a leech with your friends (never again will you call one of the girls of the Sisterhood ignominiously and whine: "Please, invite me for dinner tonight. I'll pay for everything I eat!") Your fantasy life has now been liberated, and your daydreams are technicolor, panavision, and gleefully erotic. You are free and buoyantly creative—taking up sculpture, abstract art, log-rolling, viola, swineherding, hashish, yoga, parachute-jumping, and macrobiotic balance. And, of course, now that you have lost your psychological maidenhead, you have something to talk to your headshrunk friends about, like: Now that I'm well, should I split with Mel? And, with them, you can now practice collective amateur psychiatry, asking, "That's interesting, why did you say *that?*" and interpreting everybody's behavior in terms of anal aggression, penis envy, sublimation, projection, oral imperialism, the fetal syndrome, role confusion, castra-tion, and libidinal drain, not to mention the id in yid and the oy in goy.

THE REAL PAY-OFF OF H2S

Beyond all else, H2S will teach you to cut through the banali-ties and superficialities—to get to the core of human relation-ships; feelings. The world of pure feeling, uncluttered by the surface wrappings of amenities, is of course the goal of the young, whether straight as an arrow or freaked out of the ball park. But theirs is often a false path, leading to a dead end. Thanks to therapy, you will achieve it without the necessity of taking leave of reality.

You are at a party (where in the days before therapy, the empty prattling conversation would have riveted you to the bar after you would have checked the hostess' living room for dust). The host introduces you to Dr. Somebody or other. He shakes your hand languidly and murmurs: "Gladta meetcha, dear."

In the old days, you would have returned the murmur and moved on, glass in hand and glassy of eye, to continue the sterile ritual with the other guests. But no more.

You slap his hand. "Crap," you say, brandishing your son's crap-detector. "You don't *know* me. I don't *know you*. And don't give me that cheap Hollywood—TV—politics 'dear' routine! Do you want to *communicate* or not? What do you mean you're glad to meet me? Don't hide behind such banalities— glad to meetcha, dear! We could meet a thousand times, like this, and *NEVER REALLY KNOW EACH OTHER!* It would be 'oh, how are you?' and 'nice to see you again' and 'it was good meeting you' and 'hope to see you again soon.' Look, do you *want* to know *me*? Not some unknown, blank 'dear' but *me*! Me? Okay, then, sit down. What do you *think* of me? I mean, really *think* of me! Do you think I look like Golda Meir? Say so! And what are *you* like? I mean inside, behind that mask, behind those gleaming Pepsodent teeth. Do you want a good strudel recipe? What do you think of yourself? Who are *you*? Have you been analyzed? Does it bother you that you're so short? Do you have a thing about Napoleon? What are your secret thoughts? What kind of fantasies do you have? Technicolor or just black and white? Are you embarrassed to kiss your brother on the mouth? Tell me how you symbolically killed your father. Were you toilet trained? Breast-fed? Brainwashed? Circumcised? Does a poignant poem make you cry? Can you blush? Show me! Are you *Jewish*? If you've got it, flaunt it! Is your wife Jewish? To really *KNOW* somebody you have to *give*, you have to open yourself *up*, like a cracked nut. Speak! What do you really *feel* under those layers and layers of protective skin, buried emotions and meaningless amenities that we call modern civilization? The shit is flying and all you do is turn on the fan!"

Dr. Somebody turned out to be *your* headshrinker and he got red in the face and muttered, "Really my dear, this is a bad scene!" But that's HIS problem. He couldn't stand having his defenses torn away, being made vulnerable, exposed to the nerve ends of life. He could dish it out, but he couldn't take it. You don't have to be Jewish or to experience H_2S to live with such burning intensity, but it doesn't hurt either, dear.

As to your relationship with Harold, who likewise wants only to be free, H2S will undoubtedly elevate it from intermittent irritation to pure mutual rejection ("Hello, Harold, how are you?" . . . "Get off my back, Mother!"), but at least you will know where you stand.

Which is up against the wall, Mother. Right on!

CHAPTER SEVEN

HOW TO MAKE HIM A LIBERAL, BUT NOT TOO

American Jews have a unique political tradition. Since the advent of the New Deal, Jews have been a faithful partner in the liberal coalition. Since Roosevelt, Jews have voted Democratic in higher proportions than perhaps any segment of the white community. They gave Roosevelt, Truman, Stevenson, Kennedy, Johnson and Humphrey approximately 80 per cent of their votes. (They gave Nixon 18 per cent.) In their voting behavior, as in many other group attributes, Jews are distinctive. Proportionately more Jews register and vote than do members of any other group. Whereas other ethnic groups tend to change (color them conservative) as they climb the economic ladder to middle-class affluence and suburban provincialism, the Jews in Hewlett and Westport and St. Louis Park (suburban Minneapolis) vote pretty much as they did when they lived in the Bronx, Cleveland and the north side of Minneapolis (color them liberal). The old New Deal-liberal coalition has gone bust, and relations among the old bed partners are like scorpions in a bottle. But, if and when the coalition ever gets glued together again, Jews will be working the gluepot.

Defying the sociological law of gravity in America, Jews in gilded suburban ghettos continue to cast their votes for racial justice, world peace and bold social and economic programs. Meanwhile, ironically, the laboring man (including the Jewish taxi driver) increasingly takes rightist positions on several of these, while the labor movement's foreign policy is stuck ten degrees to the right of the Chamber of Commerce. Moreover, adding to the uniqueness of the Jewish political stance, Jews are the only ethnic group which, while experiencing some of the backlash, anger and frustration which beset the entire white community at a time of severe racial conflict, does not simply vote its backlash. It must be acknowledged that elections in Minneapolis, New York and Los Angeles in 1969 showed some erosion of Jewish liberalism, but even in their eroded condition, Jews were still distinctively liberal relative to the total white community. Which, of course, says something—but not much.

Jews were probably as rattled about black militancy in 1968 as most other white ethnic groups. The difference is that many other groups voted their backlash at the polls; thus Wallace pulled a whopping 10,000,000 votes. Jews gave Wallace 1.2 per cent of their votes, a smaller percentage than any other racial or religious group except blacks. And there is the final anomaly: Jews, Exhibit A of a minority group which has made it in America, vote much like one other segment of the American population—the blacks, caged in the ghettos of American cities. Go figure.

In addition, Jews have no positive, knee-jerk reaction to Jewish candidates. If he is a Javits or a Lehman, genuine liberals, he will attract Jewish votes like a magnet. But if the other guy is a goy who seems more liberal than the Jew (Lindsay vs. Beame, Wagner vs. Lefkowitz, Johnson vs. Goldwater), the plug will be pulled on the Jewish candidate even if he wraps himself in an Israeli flag and charges across the city as if it were the Sinai Desert. Jews don't trust candidates who try to appeal to them purely on Jewish issues. The politicians who enjoyed red-hot honeymoons with Jewish voters were Roosevelt, Truman, Stevenson (especially), John F. Kennedy (not at first) and Fiorello LaGuardia—a pretty classy group of goyim.

Jewish organizations always nervously proclaim that there is no Jewish bloc vote. Well, it is true that Jews don't have bloc parties where somebody "delivers" the vote. A Jewish husband can't even "deliver" his wife's vote. But every working politician knows that there is a Jewish vote and goes out with hammer and tongs to get some chips off the old bloc.

In 1969 there was vivid evidence in the New York City election that there is no such thing as a Jewish vote. John Lindsay, the incumbent, was sat down by his political advisers who informed him, in a nutshell, that he had the blacks in his pocket, there was no way he could get the Italians or the Irish, and that the whole ballgame was, therefore, the Jews. Thereafter, John Lindsay, the paradigmatic WASP, became the most zealous Jew in town. Hardly a night went past without the televised spectacle of Mayor Lindsay, a yarmulke at the crest, davenning in at least four synagogues stretched between the Bronx and Brooklyn. When, providentially, Golda Meir (the Meir that made Milwaukee famous) came to the United States in the midst of his re-election campaign, the mayor embraced her in a bear hug so vigorous it almost wiped out Madame Prime Minister and which endured three days and three nights, shlepping her to a succah here, a museum there, here a Waldorf, there a Garden, here a snow-removal truck in Queens, there a United Nations. As Victor Borge said of John and Golda, what they had in common was that they were both up for re-election and both needed the Jewish vote, especially John, now referred to as Meir Lindsay. During the campaign, John sent a hearty mazel tov to Mayor Teddy Kollek on his re-election as mayor of Jerusalem, congratulating him from one "mishuganah" to another. Lindsay's campaign to recover the Jewish vote was obvious, transparent, ridiculous, offensive, hammish and fabulously effective. So is there a Jewish vote? Ask Mario.

Why do Jews vote like that? There are many reasons. The first reason is: why not? Jews have had a long and bitter history with anti-Semitic reaction, creating an allergy to the right. Moreover, Jewish self-interest is seen as identified with an open and enlightened society, admitting all Americans into the mainstream of a progressive nation. In addition, the Jewish religious emphasis on justice, on communal responsibility for the weak and the poor, on mercy and peace, has left its imprint even on secularized Jews. Otherwise, it would be hard to explain the disproportionate participation and leadership by Jews in all causes of civil rights, social welfare, political reform and social progress. Most Jews couldn't quote the prophets if their lives depended on it. But the fire in the belly of so many Jews, including especially Jewish youth, was not planted there by pickled herring. It was planted, through osmosis, by a

Jewish ethical stance which stems from the Jewish experience and the Jewish religion.

Of course, it is not written in the stars that Jews should be liberals in America forever. While Jewish political ideology is mostly liberal, the Jewish life-style in America is right wing already. It is sometimes said we are like everybody else, only more so, and if the country turns to the right, are Jews going to swim against the tide? Maybe. Maybe not. (Asked what he would do if the world were destroyed by flood, the Jew answered: "Learn to swim underwater.") There are already some indications of a hardening of the political arteries. For the first time in American history, some tiny groups of Jews are organizing self-defense vigilante groups to "defend" the Jewish community from black extremists and anti-Semites. Some defense! In New York City, in the wake of the ugly school conflict, a small group of Jews stood in front of Temple Emanu-El armed with baseball bats and bicycle chains, to "protect" the temple from James Forman (who didn't show up) even though the temple was already "protected" by enough New York City policemen to start a St. Patrick's Day parade. A puzzled Roman Catholic pundit remarked: "I didn't think I would ever live to see the day when New York Jews would run around like a bunch of hysterical *Brooklyn Tablet* Catholics." (All things come to those who wait.)

But most Jews are as opposed to Jewish vigilantes disguised as batmen as they are opposed to vigilantes of the right and the left, black or white, hooded or unhooded. The Jewish Defense League has a summer camp program to train young men in karate, judo and the other manly arts of self-defense. They even took out a fat ad in the New York *Times* with a picture of their mighty minions bearing clubs and pipes in front of a synagogue, with the caption: "IS THIS HOW A NICE JEWISH BOY BEHAVES?" The ad responded to its own question, saying in effect: "Hell, yes." The *Times*, still a gentle gray Jewish mother, despite everything, gave its own editorial answer: "Stop, already."

Like other organizational foolishness, the Defense League will not die but it will, hopefully, just fade away like old generals. Yet it must be admitted that it feeds on a widespread and understandable anxiety among many Jews about the use of anti-Semitism as a weapon in racial confrontations. If Jews are to be expended to mollify black rage, isn't it necessary to assert Jewish dignity through self-defense? That argument is specious because the truth is that Jews will be secure only when the entire society is healthy. But a climate of fear and uncertainty will undoubtedly help to sustain those who think the answer to our problem is to take the law into our own hands and show that nice Jewish boys will not be anybody's "patsies." But if we can do that, can't the Black Panthers? Don't ask!

While this mood of defensiveness spreads among the older members of the Jewish community, what about our youth people? What do they think? Where are they going?

Our youth people, for the most part, are going in the opposite direction. They are not a monolithic group, and all generalizations are suspect (especially this one); yet most Jewish young people *do* seem to think *we* (their parents, etc.) are "hysterical" about anti-Semitism. What do young people know about anti-Semitism? Few have ever seen it. To them, it's a terrible thing that happened before they were born and is the subject of corny old movies on the late show, like *Gentleman's Agreement*. And if an angry black teacher in Brooklyn hurls an anti-Semitic thunderbolt into the television cameras, could it be because the media just ignored him when he was merely clobbering "white honkies" in general? And they think their parents are caught up in a "Jewish bag." Even if a few anti-Semites are yapping away, isn't that dwarfed by the Vietnam war, the suppression of dissent, white racism, the decay of our cities, the fact that 30 per cent of the entering students are undercover agents for J. Edgar Hoover and that Saran Wrap (made by Dow Chemical) is permitted in the kitchen of the cafeteria? One has to have a scale of values.

So the problem with our young people is not that they will lean to the right and fall into the camp of the Jewish Birchites or vigilantes. Only a small hard core will do that, and the thing to do with them is to encourage them. If he wants to be a Minuteman, buy him a bazooka and he'll be so scared he'll head for the hills—without the bazooka.

No, your child will probably lean to the left. He will tell you that "you liberals" have loused up America, that Vietnam and the urban mess are the end products of "liberal failure," that the time has come for radical solutions. He will tell you that trying to reform the "system" from within is fruitless, as we saw in 1968. Only radical confrontations against the rotten system can achieve results in humanizing America. Since you agree that the status quo (defined as the mess we are in) is pretty bad and getting worse, how do you cope with this insurgency?

The problem for Jewish parents is both better and worse than for non-Jewish parents. Better because, by and large, Jewish parents are more sympathetic with the youthful rebellion. In the 1930s, when the Depression and Hitler dominated Jewish consciousness, many Jews were radical, some even members of the Communist Party. (When Israel was created, the Knesset, the Israeli Parliament, couldn't get any legislators to sit on the *right*.) Whereas most Americans have scared themselves half to death by the specter of "atheist Communists," most Jews have an Uncle Abe or a Cousin Dave or a neighbor Goodman, who fought in the Abraham Lincoln Brigade in Spain and/or once had chowder with Browder. (This is known as the "Red Diaper Syndrome.") These ex-Communists today are warm, soft, furry suburbanites who live in upper Westchester, keep their boats in Mamaroneck, vacation in Aruba, and revive themselves politically with an occasional anonymous check to Cleaver, Mark Rudd and the SDS. To the campus radical, the C.P. is itself one of the fat Establishments (which of course infuriates the FBI agents who have spent so many years burrowing underground in the C.P. that they have begun to look like red gophers).

One result is that Jewish young rebels are not revolting against their parents' values. They are merely taking them out of the golf club-cocktail party-barbecue-rarefied atmosphere —and applying them to life. So Jewish parents differ from WASP parents. The latter often find their college children in violent rebellion against *them* and *their* basic values; it causes hurt and shock. Jewish parents, on the other hand, feel a strange indulgent mixture of pride, guilt and understanding. (Mark Rudd's parents are as proud of Mark as the Roth parents are of Philip.) One result is that they infuriate their campus revolutionary youngsters by saying: "I *understand* you;

I'm *with* you." This is disastrous and can provoke violence. When the father is so indulgent that he melts when the son pushes against him, the son may make a *father* of his college, defy it, and make *it* the angry father he can't get at home. As Tom Lehrer says: "If you can't communicate, the least you can do is keep quiet!"

But Jews are worse off, too, because they understand that often their youthful rebels are acting out their Jewish ethical heritage. They see their daughter, Debi, as a miniskirted Deborah, confronting the injustices of our time. They see their hirsute Marvin, the campus revolutionary, as cut from the mold of Moses, the Liberator. The trouble is that the kids don't see the Jewish connection, and where they do, they conclude that, if they are Moses, then *we* are the desert generation which has got to go before the struggle can reach the Promised Land. To *you*, their Jewishness is at the core of their caring. To *them* it is incidental and unimportant. They feel linked to blacks and other oppressed peoples of the earth and don't want to get locked into a tribal bag. The romance of "struggle" not only leads some of them into weird mythologies, but it lines some of them up with black demagogues and third-world pundits whose anti-Israel antipathies cannot be distinguished from anti-Semitism. So a few Jewish parents have had the painful experience of listening to their children deifying Carmichael and Cleaver, demanding that a black anti-Semite be permitted to head a department of black studies, attacking Israel as a "tool of U.S. imperialism" and lionizing Saudi Arabia, Egypt and the Al Fatah as "socialist bastions of the Arab-liberation movement." So before you kvell about your son, the revolutionary, make sure he hasn't also become a Jewish Uncle Jake, selling out his own people for the porridge of hot rhetoric.

So now that we have limned the problem, what do we do about it? How do we cope? Don't despair. Be cool. There are techniques:

1. Give him a copy of *Portnoy's Complaint*. Better he should occupy the family bathroom than the Administration Building.

2. Send him to Israel for an extended trip (see Chapter Nine), but, in the meantime, have an Israeli student live in your house for a year. Preferably a kibbutznik. Instead of play-

ing on his guilt feelings about the holocaust or appealing to group loyalties, let your boy find out the truth that Israel is a laboratory of radical social experiment; that the kibbutz is a more successful socialist undertaking than he'll find in all of Russia, China and Berkeley combined; and that Israel is as likely to become anybody's satellite as it is to give Nasser the French gunboats as a consolation prize. Select the Israeli carefully. He should be (1) *against* the U.S. war in Vietnam; (2) in favor of doing more for the Arab refugees; (3) not a missionary for an aliyah program; (4) not an early riser; (5) a Met fan; (6) not better-looking than your own son; (7) fluent in English; (8) religious but not fanatical; (9) respectful; (10) a believer in the viability and future of the American-Jewish community. One minor hang-up is that thus far the Israeli Embassy has only produced one young Israeli who meets all of these specifications and he is now mortgaged through the year 1988.

3. Demonstrate your concern. One father we know heard that his son was demonstrating in Washington. He called the rabbi of the nearest synagogue and said: "Please, rabbi, my son, the revolutionary, is coming to your town—he's allergic to whole milk. It would be such a mitzvah if you would look after him for us!"

But the best way is to demonstrate WITH HIM! One would certainly think that being associated together in the same noble and dangerous cause would draw parent and child close together, breaking the sound barriers to communication. One father and son had traveled to the Moratorium in the same bus, but, of course, it was parents in the back of the bus. Later, the father had spent hours frigidly wandering among 300,000 peace marchers on the Mall at the Washington Monument, desperately looking for his college son. "HEY!" he exclaimed delightedly, spotting his boy. "How are you, son?" Son: "Get off my back!"

4. Send him clippings from the New York *Times*. If Cleaver denounces Zionists as "racist pigs" (a double jeopardy), clip and send without comment (to Harold, not Cleaver, dummy). If the *Times* reports the latest Soviet persecution of Jews, clip and send. If the *Times* warns that campus insurrectionaries are building up the rightniks, ditto. It is true you have sub-

scribed to the daily New York *Times* for Harold, but chances are that he reads the paper as selectively as you do.

5. The American people can be roughly divided into those who are tuned in to the movie *Graduate* and those who are tuned in to the movie *Green Berets*. Most Jews are Graduate people. Harold, without any question, is a Graduate person. So understand him, but, for heaven's sake, don't leave him alone with your sensuous friend, Mrs. Robinson, from Hadassah. Harold is not a Zionist.

6. If none of the above works, have a nice shmoos with Harold when he comes home. Wait until he is weakened by three or four days of heavy Jewish cooking. Then—casually, casually—say:

"Harold, you know your mother and I are over thirty. . . ."

"Yes, I figured that out by myself."

"And you probably think we are too old to change and too young to die. . . ."

"I didn't say that."

"Well, you know we have been *liberals* all of our lives."

"Dad, I don't hold that against you."

"And you no doubt blame us for all the evils that are still around in America and the world."

"What are you getting at, Dad?"

"I just want you to know that we do not hold with all the tactics you seem to support, though we share many of your goals."

"Well, I . . ."

"And we want you to know that we love you, even where we disagree. Love is not conditional. . . ."

"I love you, too, Dad. But love is not relevant!"

"Harold, query, in what you're doing, do you feel *Jewish?*"

"Do I feel Jewish, for Christ sake? I feel fine—a little tired from exams in Chittlings 113 Black Studies and Revolution 307, but okay."

"But are you *aware* of yourself as a Jew? I mean, your Jewish identity and all. . . ."

"Oh, I know what you want. Jewish *is* beautiful, baby.

Does that do it, Dad? Do I pass?"

"I think you *are* trying to pass. You're trying to be blacker than black and to run away from your Jewishness."

"Please, Dad, spare me . . ."

"And, while we were embarrassed when we saw your picture in the paper chasing that Dow Chemical man up a tree, we know you have to lead your own life . . ."

"I appreciate that, Dad."

"And we know you think we are really racist finks because our maid is colored, Mother is white and I have black help at the plant . . ."

"Oh, come on, Dad . . ."

"And you think we have sold out our ideals for comfort and success . . ."

"Aw, Dad, I didn't . . ."

"And you are sick of the money values of our society and the rat race of business and competition and the fleshpots of suburbia."

"Well, yes, I am . . ."

"So we want to tell you that we understand completely . . ."

"Thanks, Dad."

"And have decided to cut you out of our will so you won't be saddled with material values and be denounced by your kid, he should only be revolting like you, it will serve you right."

CHAPTER EIGHT

HOW TO KEEP HIM JEWISH, DESPITE COLLEGE

Many youngsters say, in effect, good-by God, I'm going to college. But one of the best ways to prevent such alienation from Judaism is to get your young person hooked on Judaism at an early age. Sometimes this forced feeding has a boomerang effect; in that case, duck. But some young people can be guided through the whole route—religious school, synagogue, youth group, Hillel Foundation, marrying a nice Jewish mate, raising up Jewish children and freely participating in adult Jewish life. If you have such a child, stuff him and put him up on the wall. He may soon be a rare trophy of a bygone era. But even after you have early and successfully programmed him for Jewish life, there is no guarantee that he won't bug out after the first taste of college (which is an English word for *galut* [exile]).

1. The first imperative is to plug him into a *Jewish* college. A Jewish college has nothing to do with sectarian sponsorship of the institution. Columbia is Congregationalist-sponsored, but it is Jewish. Harvard is Episcopalian but Jewish. Fordham is a Catholic School but the president is a doting Jewish mother. A Jewish college has little to do with the proportion of Jews in the student body and faculty. Big Ten schools are Jewish although some student bodies are less than 10 per cent Jewish. A Jewish college can be a large factory like Wisconsin or a small convent like Sarah Lawrence. What makes it "Jewish" is a peculiar subliminal alchemy of geography, culture, cosmopolitanism, atmosphere, black students,

climate, liberalism, a Jewish chair ("I would love to buy a chair, but must it be so upholstered?"), a Hillel Foundation and proximity to Chinese restaurants and a good deli, and an understanding that education should not interfere too much with learning. Oberlin is Jewish; Carleton is not. Beloit is Jewish; Lawrence is not. Bard is Jewish; Guilford is not. North Carolina is Jewish; South Carolina is not. Hunter College is now run by a former nun but she is married to a Jew! Brandeis is parve (neutral). You really need a score card, but unfortunately there are none. So do the next best: read the chapter on "How to Get Harold into College" in the authoritative volume, *My Rabbi Doesn't Make House Calls.*

When you were young, the quota system against Jews in college was still formidable. In recent years, religious discrimination at college has been largely swept away, although some Midwestern colleges are now slapping new quotas on Eastern (read Jewish) students. Thanks to fair-educational-practice laws, and the determination of minority youngsters with good heads, the doors are wide-open to the qualified (especially if they are black and poor). Competition for the best schools is fierce, but remember that the definition of a "good" school is the one that admits your child, who in turn asks: Why do we have to degrade ourselves, why shouldn't the colleges apply to us *kids?*

2. Now that he or she is admitted, don't plop back into a chair and think the task is over. *Au contraire.* Your job is only just begun. Making him think it was *HIS* choice is the next step (and keeping him *in* college is no cinch, either). After that, you must persuade Harold that he should be accompanied to freshman orientation; and to persuade your husband that he should do the accompanying. This is clever of you because you know that Harold would balk at letting YOU go with him and, once he is well briefed, your husband will adequately discharge the functions of a seeing eye dog. Your husband must play it cool or he will drive Harold out of his skull, right out of school and into the arms of the Draft Board, heaven forfend. If it is handled properly, the orientation will give your son and husband an opportunity to get "reacquainted" and, chances are, with Dad on his nerves, Harold won't realize how irrelevant is his Alma Mater (which is Latin

for Blessed are those who run around in circles for they shall be called Big Wheels).

Orientation will be a drag, and Harold will not learn much that is serviceable, but Dad will learn a great deal about himself. His wife having stayed home so that their son wouldn't be embarrassed by the clucking of a solicitous mother at his college baptism, Harold's father will be astonished to find that HE is also a Jewish mother! Just listen to him: "Put on your windbreaker, for God's sake, you'll catch your death!!" "Tonight you're going to take a shower!" "Listen, it wouldn't hurt you to put on your hello tag like everybody else!" "Whaddayamean you won't have any breakfast, you can't take tests on an empty stomach." "Please, please, don't give me a heartache; at least let the barber give you a trim." In this setting, terrible role confusion ensues. Mostly in Dad. He behaves as if he is Harold's mother, but deep down he also believes he is his own *son*, tremulous with the excitement of a wondrous new world opening up for him. He is back in college again, big man on campus, irresistible to the girls, bantering and gay, and brilliant withal. It is like reincarnation. Once, while his son is being tested, he tests himself by yielding himself up to a youthful fantasy. He fixes a miniskirted coed with a playful nod. She smiles! And takes his elbow and leads him across the street, nodding.

The orientation consists of extended testing of the new freshmen, followed by preregistration for fall classes. Meanwhile, Dad and the other parents are subjected to "orientation" from 8:30 A.M. to 10 P.M., learning a great deal more about the college than they really care to know. The orientation consists of fourteen lectures by the director of pacification, explaining away the "little trouble" we had during recent months. (Only four buildings burned down, 100 students maced, 500 arrested, and two university presidents AWOL). The orientation lectures are preceded by a tour of the new buildings built in "modern riot architecture" (all steel, no glass).

The usual lecture goes like this: "If your son or daughter gets arrested, he or she will receive due process, which is a hell of a lot better than your sons and daughters will give us, I'll tell you. Now you've been hearing and reading about all the troubles here on campus, and you probably imagine that this place is infested with hippies and yippies, revolutionaries, anarchists, police and potheads. It is. But education goes on regardless. Our big problem is the damned media. They don't care about the 10,000 kids who go about their business, getting an education. Does TV ever report on the planes that are *not* hijacked? They only care about violence and disruption. Why, once some student militants marched up the hill here to burn a flag and I persuaded them that was not the way to make their point. But they had to go through with it because they had notified the press and TV, and there were 57 varieties of cameras, network and local, to immortalize that puff of smoke, stamping their feet and shouting at the kids: 'YOU PROMISED! YOU PROMISED!' We made Huntley and Brinkley that night. One other time we made Cronkite and 'The Today Show.' Does anybody here know how to get to Johnny Carson by any chance? We are not as well known as Berkeley, Harvard, or Columbia, but we are getting on the map. We now have the biggest student body in the region—one fourth of the students are from out of state, not including police undercover agents."

Actually, Dad and Harold will learn a lot more just moseying about the campus and talking to students informally than they will learn from the formal orientation. The following is a verbatim account of a casual conversation they had with a sweet young girl who was working in a campus bookstore:

"Do you like it here?"

"Compared to what?"

"I mean, should we believe all those things we've been reading in the papers about the university?"

"Not unless you read the Berkeley *Barb*, the Goucher *Goose*, or the Radcliffe *Ream!*"

"Well, let's be more specific. Is there a serious pot problem here?"

"No problem at all. You can get it anywhere."

"I see. Well, is it true that boys and girls are sleeping together in dormitories?"

"Of course. What's your thing—boys and boys? That's fine, too. Consenting adults and all that jazz . . ."

"Well, reading the paper, you get the feeling that there's so much trouble and excitement on campus that students have no time for studies. Is that true?"

"Not yet, but I think this will be a better year. We have big plans."

"You work here in the bookstore. Can you tell us what equipment to buy so my son will be ready for school in the fall?"

"A gas mask. A bullhorn. A pith helmet. A jock strap. Track shoes. A copy of Fanon's *The Wretched of the Earth. Quotations from Chariman Mao.* And some Ex-Lax."

"Ex-Lax? Why Ex-Lax?"

"Watsamatter, man, you don't want your son to join the Movement?"

HOW TO KEEP HIM JEWISH THOUGH COLLEGIATE

3.   In the joyful but frantic and kaleidoscopic task of raising your children—including the car pools, piano lessons, daily lists of chores, PTA meetings, conferences with teachers whose teeth are on edge, whirlwind shopping, the whole shmeer— one thing which will keep you going is the certain knowledge that one day they will grow up and go off to college. *Then,* you and your mate can relax and discover each other. *Then,* the telephone, bathroom, TV, stereo, and living room will be available to *you. Then,* there will be time to shift gears— time for travel, leisure, conversation, friendships, parties, tennis, long-postponed courses at the New School, painting, sculpture, books, Weight Watchers, baseball, folk dancing, theater, con- certs, vacations, and just sitting down doing nothing and with- out a goddamn *list.*

Well, here we are. Today, your children are off to college. Liberation has dawned. It is V-day. The investment of your- self over seventeen years has finally produced its rich dividend. They're gone. The stereo plays your own soft Mozart. All that's left of them is a long-distance voice on Sunday evening. The bedrooms are empty. How do you feel? *Heartbroken,* that's how! Like every other parent, you can't take yes for an answer. Well, now that they're in college, at least we can worry about how to communicate with them and to keep them Jewish. It's not as nerve-racking as having them home but it's better than nothing.

HOW TO COMMUNICATE

4. Such things as participating in your son's orientation
help parents to learn the jargon without which it is impossible
to communicate with college students. Since you are an over-
age square, you must take pains to learn the new language, in
which every sentence begins with "like" and ends with "mother."
It is hard to learn, but it comes with practice. Here is the
transcript of a telephone conversation between a hip father
and his college son which was, of course, bugged by a bell-
bottomed FBI informer and which has come into our hands
by foul means:

> Father: "Like hello there, Sylvan. Where's it at? Your mother
> and I are real uptight because we just saw on the boob tube
> that the pigs are macing you cats at Berkeley. It's a bad scene,
> and I wanted to know if my son, the revolutionary, is where
> the action's at."
>
> Son: "Hello, Dad."
>
> F: "Like you campus cats are really blowing their minds, those
> fascist pigs, and they keep saying you're all stoned—you know,
> putting you all in one bag, Sylvan baby. What are you *into*,
> Man?"
>
> S: "I'm fine, Dad."
>
> F: "That's right, Sylvan. Just tell it like it is. Up against the
> wall with all those goddamn hypocritical mothers. Right, son?"
>
> S: "How *is* Mom, Dad?"
>
> F: "Mom? You mean the Mother? I'll tell you like it is. Like
> she's scared shitless, man! She took one look at the boob tube
> and she like freaked out yelling: 'They're gonna bust my Sylvan,'
> and then she got hold of herself and we joined hands here in
> the living room and we sang 'WE SHALL OVERCOME.'
> Are you really okay, Sylvan?"
>
> S: "Fine, Dad."
>
> F: "Groovy, man. Groovy. Like were you out there in the street
> when the vitamin governor with the flipped-out skull sent that

crummy helicopter, wow, to mace you down? But you socked it to him, right, son?"

S: "No, Dad, I was studying."

F: "Studying? Oh. Like that's it, man, I dig you! Just do your own thing, right? That's out of sight!"

S: "What's out of sight, Dad?"

F: "You're putting me on, Sylvan. Beautiful! What's that, operator? Like our three minutes are up, wow, man, we gotta split now. It's been a gas, communicating with you like this. I mean, how many old cats can rap with their kids?"

S: "So long, Dad . . . And good night, J. Edgar."

It is crucial for parents to be able to talk like this father because nothing will turn off the young faster. And that is a hell of a lot better than trying to communicate with them.

5. Espionage.

It is vital to keep track of what your son or daughter is experiencing in college—his thoughts, impressions, liaisons, loves, doubts, aspirations, problems, and personal development. This information will permit you to measure the gravitational pull, if any, of your parental teachings. But how will you find out? He will never tell you anything but rank and serial number. There is one solution: espionage. You can listen in on his telephone conversations when he's home. ("Get off the phone, Dad.") You can hire his roommate, or bug his dorm, or buy the services of Mitchell Hoover, the double agent who is an undercover campus narcotics agent (disguised as a beaded homosexual hippie), who moonlights by selling information to anxious parents. He has uncovered more secret documents than the Pentagon and, like the Pentagon, the documents always prove what you want to establish. For a mite extra, Hoover will also decipher the four-letter words into English for you.

Another way—which works only rarely—is to give Harold a diary. If you are lucky, Harold will keep it daily. Then the trick is to rifle his luggage when he comes home to visit or, failing that, have Mitchell Hoover borrow it every fortnight and photostat it for you. (While he is at it, Hoover will also sell copies to the Dean of Students, rival political factions on campus, the FBI, the Narcotics Bureau, the Draft Board, Spiro

Agnew, Martha Mitchell, CIA, and the New York *Daily News* for its latest exposé of college scandals.)

Let's assume that Harold does keep a diary. It might read like this:

September 7—

First day school. Assigned to Merrill Hall, near the lake. Groovy. Roomate, Unga Shtup, a shmuck from Seattle. He was a Bennington coed who sought sanctuary here! He is apparently a leader of the Maoists and he has pictures of Chairman Mao all over the walls and he has taken over the closet as an arsenal for making Molotov cocktails to use against the SDS. Right away he called me a "Bourgeois liberal" and we almost came to blows. He's a sour apple, low level of cosmic cheer. Took me four hours to unpack the suitcases mom packed for me. Where can I keep five kosher salamis, for God sake? And would you believe *THREE* Union Prayerbooks? And an entire set of the Jewish Encyclopedia? Unga took one look, rolled his eyes, and denounced me as a "cosmopolitan chauvinist." Spent time getting myself oriented. It's thirty miles to the nearest track, seven miles to the ball park, and a mile to the nearest pub. Cut classes. What a drag!

September 25—

Sorry, diary, long time no see. Been too much going on in campus. Paul Boreigas, an SDS hot shot, disrupted classes today, wearing the head of a pig, denouncing the "umbilical connections between the university and the Pentagon." I wasn't in class, but hurried over when I telephoned Dial-A-Demonstration and got the word. Seems the university has accepted a Pentagon contract to study the sex habits of the Chinese war lords between 1910–20. Boreigas is a ballsy guy. I understand he once had charisma, but he was treated for it. He wears braces on his teeth to get out of the draft. ("I could set off a whole mine-field.") He demanded that all students "get their shit together," whatever that means. Paul was heaved out of class by the Black Panthers who insisted they had planned their own disruption for that hour and denounced Paul as a "deviationist honkie fink," whatever that is. Anyway, the university suspended Paul. Tonight there was a really fab

demonstration outside the Administration building demanding
due process for Paul. Things are looking up. Tomorrow, all
things being equal, I plan to go to classes and meet my teachers,
unless something is happening on campus.

September 26—

Things are not equal. The joint is swinging. Out of sight,
man! Josh Midriff was elected chairman of the Ad Hoc Committee for Due Process for Paul Boreigas. Josh is pretty stupid,
and I think he's a/c d/c, but he has access to a mimeograph
machine so he's a student leader. At 3 P.M. today, the Committee occupied the Administration building and organized a
commune. I joined in because I wanted to find out what a
commune is. It's where everybody sits on the floor, gets drunk
on beer, calls each other brother and sister, sings madrigals,
and urges each other to get our own shit together. It's a beautiful scene. Administration got sweated and gave us an ultima-
tum: get out by 4 P.M. or face suspension. I began to sweat
a lot; I really got my sweat together. At 3:45, the Afro-Students
Union sent us a message that we were diverting revolutionary
energy from their black demands, that we were counterrevolu-
tionary racist pigs, and that if we didn't get our asses out by
3:55, they would throw us out. The logic was very persuasive
to me, and, while the Ad Hockers were debating the message,
I slipped out the side window and shimmied down the drain-
pipe right behind the iron-assed dean of men. I am more
interested in black power than due process anyway. Tomorrow
I really MUST get to class. Six letters from Mom and Dad,
urging me to drop in at Hillel House and also attaching the
phone numbers of five nice Jewish girls in town. Mom writes
she is watering my plant; hope she doesn't find out what it is.

October 2—

I have been working with the Afro-Students Union. That's
where the action is, except the really avant-garde students are
dropping race and peace for Indians and pollution. We are
making 19 non-negotiable demands, but at the big confrontation with the Administration today, one of the black leaders,
Mau 37X, turned to me and growled: "Honkie, why don't
you go and do your own thing? Go fight racism in suburbia.

Let us get our own black shit together, man. We gotta find
out who we blacks are, our own identity, history, heritage, the
whole shmeer. How can we do that if you honkies keep shlepping us to the ice cream shoppe and the library to show off
your integrationism? Go feel virtuous somewhere else. Get off
our backs, Whitey. Get yourself a new toy! Do your OWN
THING!" Felt rejected. Wandered back to the Ad Hockers
but Paul has been given due process, has been reinstated, and
everybody has a case of the blahs. It's a drag. They want to
confront the Establishment but about what? We'll have to
wait three weeks for the Marine recruiter to come to campus.
One cat suggested everybody cut ½ inch off his IBM cards
and "screw-up the computer." Another suggested burning our
draft board. But we didn't dig these ideas, knowing that every
one of them was planted by Jacque Fagel, CIA agent pro-
vocateur. So it looks like back to classes (wherever THEY
are), which everybody agrees are not relevant and interfere
with education.

If the blacks have to find out who they are, who am I?
What am I? What IS my own thing? Strolled over to the
Hillel Foundation, it would have made Mom and Dad very
happy. Found 12 Jewish cats, mostly straight arrows and vita-
mins, all of whom had been rejected by the black cats, and
we organized a gung-ho Jewish Liberation Movement on the
spot. We went into town to a body-painting studio and had
our bodies painted like Chagall Windows. I'm Naftali. Then we
had buttons made : "Ruach is Jewish soul!" Tomorrow we draw
up our own Jewish non-negotiable demands.

October 5—

Today we presented our Jewish non-negotiable demands to
the Administration:

1. An autonomous department of Jewish studies (to include
    a full listing of all Jewish craters on the moon, in-
    cluding the Rabbi Levi, a large crater in the fourth
    quadrant named after Levi Ben Gershon who lived from
    1288 to 1344 and invented a device for astronomical
    observation; Abenezra, a big crater named after Abra-
    ham Ben Meir Ibn Ezra, a Spanish rabbi who invented
    the "keli hanehoshet," whatever that is, which meas-

ured the altitude of the sun; the Jacobi, a crater named after a German-Jewish mathematician; and several other Jewish craters most of whom are located in the fourth quadrant, a quiet neighborhood near transportation).

2. A separate but better kosher dining hall
3. A mezuzah on every door
4. Tea in a glass in the cafeteria
5. Inclusion of the hora in the senior prom
6. An annual observance of Sammy Davis Jr.'s birthday to be jointly sponsored by the Jewish Liberation Movement and the Afro Students Union and to be entitled "FELT MIR TSORES (I don't have enough troubles?) DAY"
7. A weekly shmoose by each student with the President, who should be a Jewish mother
8. Begin all classes ten minutes late
9. The University should plant a grove of trees in Israel
10. Move the University to a better neighborhood in the suburbs.

As I feared, the demands were referred to a special committee of the Senate which, unfortunately, has been locked into Communications Hall for the past seven months by the P.O., whoever they are. Unless we can persuade the blacks that our Jewish demands are relevant, I'm afraid we can't hack it!

October 20—

Today I sold out. Went to classes. Classes not relevant. Relevance is irrelevant. Felt guilty sitting there except got good vibrations from a chick sitting next to me. Fatima Palmer. She's into the astrology bit and freaked out when she learned I was Aquarius. Told me she has been putting LSD into the lake every day and thinks she is gradually turning on the whole university. Is she putting me on? She's a swinger. Is she Jewish? It would be narrow to ask. But I'd better find out before Mom swoops in here on Visitors Day and zaps me!

October 27—

Well, diary, today it all hit the fan. Instead of class, I took Fatima out on the lake in a canoe and we got into deep water.

Turns out she's some kind of liquid nymphomaniac. The lake turns her on! "Don't worry," she says, "I'm on the pill," (did she mean LSD or birth control?) and she dives at me, upsetting the canoe, and I had to swim three miles for dear life with Fatima Australian-crawling up my back, muttering, "C'mon, right here in the water, Aquarius." It was a hairy scene, and I was almost liquidated. I hid in the woods for three hours, under a camouflaged bazooka gun, until she wandered away on the false scent of a campus jock she had been laying for for some time. College *is* dangerous!

Back to the quadrangle to find a full-fledged riot in progress, gas bombs exploding, the pigs macing the cats without regard to race or rank, and a helicopter lifting the university president to exile. Apparently what happened was that some creep provoked the uprising by coming into campus with a package of Saran Wrap which, as any fool knows, is made by Dow Chemical. The riot radicalized the entire student body, including me, and we all threw off our clothes and, naked, defiant and liberated, skinny-dipped collectively in the lake (joined by four cops who had become overheated if not radicalized). What a fantastic, psychedelic, exultant, and spiritual scene, I thought, when, *voila*, Fatima emerged like a beached whale, seized my left foot, dragged me to the foggy bottom and deflowered me in the deep before I could even find out if she is Jewish.

Memo

To: *Mom and Dad*

Copy: *FBI, Narcs, Draft Board, University Administration, and Dormitory Mother*

Subject: *My Diary*

I know why you gave me this diary. No doubt, having read the above entries, you are having a cow. Relax, it's a put on! I made it all up so you could see how it could have been worse and so you won't get too burned when you learn that I'm transferring to Bennington where the boys are the coeds, the ratio is one coed to every ten chicks, and that is a hell of a lot more relevant than education!

Harold.

CHAPTER NINE

HOW TO SEND HIM TO ISRAEL

If all else fails, send Harold to Israel, for heaven's sake. You can send him to work on a kibbutz (collective farm). You can enroll him at the Hebrew University for a year. You can smuggle him into a UJA young leaders delegation. (All he has to do is ask: "Tell me, what is JEWISH about Israel?") You can enter him into a Bible contest. (He'll get eliminated in the first round when he puts Joshua into the whale, but at least he'll be in Eretz.) He can go there on a quickie trip with a notebook and announce after the second day that he is writing a book on Israel to be entitled *Israel—Yesterday, Today, and Tomorrow.* He can also get there, all-expenses-paid, if he is a radical third-world anti-Israel youth, especially if he is black, and still better if he is a hot-eyed Black Panther clergyman. Israel has a thing about converting its enemies, and they will pay him to go in order to pay him later to make pro-Israel speeches in Richmond, Virginia.

One way for Harold to get to Israel is to be a tour leader and shepherd a flock of tourists from America. The leader usually gets a free ticket or, if he is a rabbi, his congregation may give him a one-way ticket. Because of the euphoria which grips Jews in going to Israel, the diverse members of the group can be expected to subordinate their petty concerns and minor irritations—until they get to the airport. The leader conducts his happy group throughout Israel, all the while answering such questions as: How come Goldberg has a balcony and I've got a broom closet? How could you bring us to Jerusalem on Shabbat—they take in the sidewalks? Tell me, is everybody in this kibbutz Jewish? Don't any Israelis dance the hora? How could you have permitted the plane to land in Greece (fascist), France (Pompidou) or Germany (nazis) en route to Israel? How come I had a virus and took a pill with water and lost the virus and was sick three days from the water? Is it true that Israel has no House of Lords because no Jew would admit the nobility of another Jew? So this is Caesaria? If they didn't have enough money to finish, they shouldn't have started building. Is it true you specialize in unescorted elderly women?

The leader from the United States is the organizer, administrator and therapist who spends his days massaging the egos of his constituents and leading them on and off the tour bus. The actual guide (*madrich*) is an Israeli, a true Renaissance man who talks twelve languages, knows every relic (pronounced "re-*lick*") in this Renaissance land and has more diplomacy at his fingertips than Abba Eban. He is less likely to be driven out of his skull than is the American leader who is not trained in *savlanut* (which is Hebrew for "patience" and is accompanied by a hand gesture of infinite expressiveness). He can squeeze three thousand years of history out of five days like toothpaste.

Arrangements must be played by ear and the leader must be in daily telephone conversation with Franny's Tours about plans for the morrow. One leader was at a kibbutz in Galilee with his little tribe and he made a call to the tour office in Tel Aviv to review details for the next day. When he said something about picking up the group's mail, the Tel Aviv operator broke in: "Concerning *that*, I should like to say a few words."

One "leader" had in his charge a lovely group of Californians, including Mr. and Mrs. Isaiah Lot from Beverly Hills. Mr. Lot was a big diaper manufacturer; Mrs. Lot was an eight-cylindered yenta who always could be relied on to keep the tour bus waiting, to stop the bus on the hour for toilet calls, never to accept her room and—because her Aquarius son asked her to bring home some shells from the beach—to shlepp home a bazooka, howitzer and 155 mm. shells not to mention the three El Al bags filled with rock and sand. Her husband became increasingly agitated as she stimulated near-hysteria among the group. When the bus stopped at desolate Sodom and everyone got out to look at the potash works, the guide shouted to Mrs. Lot, who was stuffing the salty sand into her El Al bag, "Don't look back, Mrs. Lot!"

Of course, she turned back just in time to see Mr. Lot, his face relaxed and serene, leap into the bus, drive it madly across the Jordanian border, shrieking wildly like the Texas pilot in *Dr. Strangelove*, shouting "Shalom! Shalom! Free at last, oh, God Almighty, free at last!"

Your son will arrive in Israel as a typical American tourist, kissing the ground, loving everybody, crying a lot, seeing everything through the prism of the golden sentimentality with which you endowed him. He'll be awed by the beauty of the land and the openness, the directness, the spirit, the positive values, the élan and the unity of the people. However, as is the human condition everywhere, the longer his stay, the more critical he will become. The Hollywood panavision glow will dissolve under the close-up of daily life. The picture-postcard Israel will give way to the flesh-and-blood reality with human blemishes, warts, whiskers and all. Like the Israelis themselves, he will strip away the sentimental conceits and see the deeper, truer glory of the real Israel, acne and everything. In the process, of course, he will explode the following myths—and near-myths—which are part of the American-Jewish tourist's baggage about Israel:

1 WHY DOES THE UNITED STATES HAVE SUCH TROUBLE INTE-GRATING THE RACES WHEN YOUNG ISRAEL HAS INTEGRATED EVERY-BODY IN SIGHT?

Israel has indeed done a remarkable job in achieving unity and molding many polyglot groups, coming from every corner of the earth, into one nation. Thanks especially to the Israeli Army, Israelis from divergent cultures are quickly absorbed into Israeli life. But the millennium has not yet arrived. Israel is a land of many tribes. Some Israelis acknowledge "two Israels" —one European-Ashkenazi and the other Oriental-Sephardic; the first advantaged and the second deprived. A French-speaking Jew (who may have come from Morocco and whose sole contact with France may have consisted of one memorable night in Paris en route elsewhere) will be asked to "explain" Pompidou. An American Jew who came to Israel to settle ten years ago will be referred to as an "Anglo-Saxi" and will be called upon by his coworkers to explain what "your idiot State Department" is up to now. A Rumanian Jew, who escaped persecution in Bucharest to make his life in Israel, will find himself congratulated for the "courageous stand *you* have taken in establishing diplomatic relations with Israel."

German Jews are labeled "yeckes," while Yiddish-speaking Jews are called "vus vus." (Their standard reply to anything said to them in Hebrew is "Vus? Vus?"—which means "What? What?".) The yecke is likely to look down his nose at the Polish Jew who looks askance at the Rumanian Jew who views the Russian Jew with disdain. An Egyptian Jew lacks the status of the elite Sephardic family, but he has more yichus than a Moroccan Jew. An Iraqi Jew is still lower down in the pecking order and Kurdish Jews are regarded as "primitiv." Young sabras don't care much about these "tribal" distinctions; they join in a universal sense of superiority to their fellow Jews in the Diaspora, especially those in the United States. The ambivalence of Israelis toward American Jews is implicit in the Israeli's contempt for the "Zionists" who prate about Zion but refuse to settle in Israel. But when they *do* settle in Israel, Israelis ask them, "Tell me, why would you leave America to come live HERE?" Israel is a modern miracle, but a melting pot it isn't. It's more like a boiling stew—savory, strong and barely digestible.*

Pre-1948 settlers make up the elite Israeli "Mayflower" generation. Some American Jews who settled permanently in Israel found their sabra kids grew up speaking flawless Hebrew, wincing at their parents' labored Hebrew and regarding their parents as modern greenhorns. All these caste and pedigree distinctions are held in fairly good check, thanks to the continuing and overriding crisis. But could Israel survive if peace broke out?

The harder problem of integration is your son, Harold. Some sabras will resent him—his money, his opportunities, his failure to settle permanently in Israel. And Harold may come to love Israel and dislike Israelis. The Hebrew University will organize "Take an American to Lunch" affairs, dialogues, seminars,

* Some of this material is based on the perceptive observations of Leon Fine in his book *An American in Israel*, published in 1970 by the Israel Publishing Company.

workshops and coffee klatches, which both the Americans and Israelis will avoid in droves, proving that they do *indeed* have something in common.

2   ISRAEL IS SUCH A SMALL COUNTRY (ABOUT THE SIZE OF NEW JERSEY BEFORE IT WAS SOLD TO THE MAFIA) THAT IT DOESN'T HAVE THE GEOGRAPHICAL RIVALRIES THAT DIVIDE A COUNTRY LIKE AMERICA.

You should live so long. The rivalries among Israeli cities make the competitiveness between San Francisco and Los Angeles, or St. Paul and Minneapolis, look like *kinderspiel*. Jerusalem is one of the most magnificent cities in the world, but to the people of bustling Tel Aviv it is a dull and provincial town. Eternal City—eternal speeches! To Jerusalemites, Tel Aviv is an embarrassment—raucous, dirty, nervous and commercial. The people of the splendid city of Haifa agree with the invidious comments of both. To them there is only one true city in Israel which is comparable in grandeur to Rio and Naples and San Francisco. Besides, they say, "our buses run on the Sabbath." Yes, reply the Tel Avivis, "but tell me, to where have the buses got to go?" C'mon, say the Jerusalemites, we are the reunited heart of Israel and your own residents can't wait to come to the Western Wall and to walk through the Old City! The kibbutzniks, while advertising for recruits in the city papers, dismiss all the city-dwellers as bourgeois fat cats.

Your prodigal son, of course, will resolve the problem in his own way. He will live in none of these places. Instead, to the utter consternation of the Israelis, he will move into a spacious villa (for 150 Israeli pounds a month, which is $50 American money) in the all-Arab village of Bethany, getting along famously with his Arab neighbors while terrorist incidents ignite all the borders. Your son has blundered into the safest spot in all of greater Israel; what Al Fatah is going to attack an all-Arab village? What a Yiddishe kop your son has!

3   ISRAELI YOUTH ARE NOT REBELLING.

Israel has no indigenous hippies (only imports). Nobody knows why this is. The United States Office of Education has done research in Israel, seeking to learn why Israeli youth are less alienated than American youth; and why it is that hippies do not flourish on Israeli soil. The researchers were two Ph.D. hippies from San Francisco State, who padded barefoot throughout Israel, wearing Chanukah bushes on their heads, murmuring "wow, groovy, man" at everything they saw. Their conclusion was that hippies, like tobacco, cannot flourish in Israel's rocky soil. They hypothesized that hippies grow in alienated cultures, but how can hippies emerge in a country with 2,000,000 presidents, all of them Jewish mothers? The research project ended badly as the two bearded researchers were co-opted by the Naturei Karta, an ultra-Orthodox group in Jerusalem, and were arrested for stoning two American tourists taking photographs on the Sabbath. As Harold wrote you, this gives Israel a negative image!

It's a damn good thing that Israeli students are NOT in revolt against the universities and the Establishment. If Israeli students *did* revolt, Israel wouldn't survive one day. American universities only have to contend with a bunch of raunchy youngsters who don't want ROTC. Israeli students consist of jaunty jet pilots, cocky artillery colonels, salty commodores ("by me you're a commodore, my son, but by a commodore are you a commodore?"), dashing paratroopers and twenty-year-old infantry generals. As your son will testify, Israeli youth are not rebellious, but many are revolting.

4   ISRAELIS ARE AMONG THE MOST CULTURED PEOPLES OF THE WORLD, WITH AN EXTRAORDINARY REPERTORY THEATER, OPERA HOUSE, AND FIRST-RATE DANCE COMPANIES.

True, but the real passion of Israelis (and of Harold) is movies—any movies, including John Wayne Westerns and Arab melodramas. Is there any other country in the world where scalpers operate in front of motion-picture houses as if the Super Bowl was inside? Is there any other country in the world where motion pictures are interspersed with commercials which the audience boos and applauds? Seeing a movie in Israel is a unique experience, but the best show is not on the screen. Harold spends delightful evenings without even looking at the screen. The voices of the actors are barely audible over the thunder of "garineem" (poppy seeds) being cracked throughout

the theater, and heads are in danger of being cracked by irate
movie-goers insisting that some "idiot" is sitting in their seats,
and all this amidst the cacophony of transistor radios announcing the latest news and the babble of informal interpreters
deciphering the Hebrew (or English, French or Russian sub-
titles) into Yiddish or some other language for the benefit of
a neighbor who doesn't dig the language on the screen. *La
Traviata* in Hebrew is delicious, but an evening at the movies
is unforgettable, like a day with the old New York Mets before
they were destroyed by success. Harold was a movie buff in the
States—but seeing a movie in the U.S. compared to Israel, is
like kissing a girl through a handkerchief!

5   ISRAEL IS THE ONLY TRUE DEMOCRACY IN THE MIDDLE
EAST, GRANTING FULL POLITICAL AND RELIGIOUS FREEDOM TO ALL.

The "religious question" really turns Harold on. He writes
about the "Datican" (the name Israelis give to the Ministry of
Religion). "Dati" means "religious" which, in Israel, means
Orthodox Judaism. Most Israelis are not religious (the true
religion of Israel is Israel), but they feel that if they were, they'd
be Orthodox. Israel grants full religious freedom to all—except
some Jews, including *guess who.* This is because the political
coalitions in Israel are so precarious that every government has
had to make concessions to the Orthodox political parties. The
result? Harold writes you about a rabbinical ruling that forbade
the marriage of a Jew named Cohen to a divorced woman. The
Jew happened to be a justice of the Israeli Supreme Court and
he was a descendant of the ancient priestly cast of Cohens and,
thus, was forbidden by Orthodox religious law from marrying
his fiancée. The Justice and his woman had to find justice in
New York, where they were finally married.

In 1970 the Israeli Supreme Court tangled with the thorny
question, who is a Jew? by answering, in a 5 to 4 vote: Who
isn't?

A rabbi in Israel can black-list a hotel that has the chutzpah
to hold a forum on the Sabbath. A Reform or Conservative rabbi
cannot bury or marry his own members in Israel; only an
Orthodox rabbi has legal authority—or a non-Jewish clergyman.
This un-Jewish denial of religious liberty will not long be

countenanced in Israel. A hopeful sign of the changing times occurred in 1969 when the courts ordered the Israeli television stations to go on the air on the Sabbath, providing entertainment to Israelis, despite the dour warnings of the Datican. Harold wanted to be a Sabbath sit-in at the TV studio, but they couldn't understand his Hebrew so he quit in disgust. While the children of Israel watch television, who can doubt that Golda, the most famous Jewish mother in the world, will bring *sholom bayis* (peace in the house) among the feverish siblings of this intense Jewish family so that some day a Reform rabbi will perform a wedding on the Johnny Carson show?

6 ISRAEL IS THE MOST EFFICIENT DEMOCRATIC NATION IN THE MIDDLE EAST.

This isn't saying much. Efficiency is heresy in this part of the world. Efficiency and the Middle East are mutually exclusive. The Arab wheels move on baksheesh; the Israeli on WASP (see quiz at conclusion of this chapter).

Israel is the only democratic country in the Middle East, but efficient? Just as the Mafia is the most efficient aspect of American life, so the only efficient part of Israel is the army. An army that can fly out the enemy's radar station could also bring home the Sphinx and the pyramids! Every other bureaucracy is *farblundjet* (mixed up) in a typically Israeli brand of delightful chaos. Let Harold try to buy a car, rent a flat, or organize a dig without the proper papers. They will get Harold so unstrung he won't know whether he is coming or going—this is also how they handled the Arabs all these years.

Or let Harold shlepp to the post office to send a package back to the States. There are four long lines. (Queueing up is a way of life in Israel.) Harold gets on one line, fending off elbows fore and aft. The lines move slowly; Harold is patient. He finally gets to the clerk at the table. Harold explains, in English, he wants to send a package to the States. "Go next line," the clerk says. "He speak English."

Harold gets on the end of another line. He considers making it a point of personal privilege to go to the front, having already endured one line. But he knows he would be flayed alive. So he waits. Finally he gets to the English-speaking clerk, who says, "You want this insured?" Harold says yes. "Then go to line three."

Wearily, Harold goes to line 3—a longer line. He finally navigates that line, using the time to summon up his broken Hebrew and inflict it upon the clerk: "Ani rotzeh—ha-package ha-ze—insurance." The clerk, irritated: "Lo, lo, go line one." Which is just where Harold had begun. Indignant, Harold explodes in English: "That's where I was; he sent me here and I'm staying here!"

Now Clerk 3 and Clerk 1, who belong to rival political parties, retire behind a railing to argue out this jurisdictional dispute, puncturing the air with "idiot" and gestures, while one hundred Israelis join vehemently in the controversy. It is finally settled, but, unfortunately, it is time to close, the windows are rattled down, and Harold makes plans to spend tomorrow at the post office.

What distinguishes the Israeli is the savage glee he derives from roasting his own bureaucracy. Never in all of history has a people so beleaguered and threatened on all sides drawn such strength from laughing at the foibles and follies of that great big Yiddish Disneyland called Israel.

7   ISRAEL'S IMAGE IS ERODING.

The problem is that everybody loved Israel when it was an underdog, but now that it is a winner, a top dog, Israel has lost the sympathy of much of the world. The world understands Jews as victims—but not Jews militarily triumphant! Israel brought this public relations crisis upon itself. If it had had the sense to lose the six day war, Israel's image in the world would be beautiful today. There would be ecumenical memorial services everywhere, specially commissioned sculptures entitled "Holocaust Two" and great weeping and breast-beating at the United Nations about "the crime of silence." There would be a short-lived Broadway sensation by Rolf Hochuth entitled *The Secretary General and Other People in Glass Houses*, and the yiddish version would be called *Nu, U, Nu?* (Your Harold, of course, would wait for the movie version.)

But, Israel, shortsighted as it indubitably is, not only survived—but won every war. Can world opinion countenance Jews as occupiers, Jews as fighters, Jews as powerful, Jews as upper dogs? Decidely no! So the New Left looks down its nose at Israel as a relic of "bourgeois capitalism," many Christian leaders find unforgivably gauche Israel's refusal to disappear into history, some black spokesmen sneer at Israel as "kosher nationalism" tied to white racist imperialism, and many Jewish youth, including your Harold, view Israel with glacial indifference. (The existence of Israel is a matter of indifference to him, but the idea of the *non-existence of* Israel is unthinkable and makes Harold come on like "Gang Busters!") The Israelis know that becoming Biafrans could solve their public relations problem instantly, but they go on their stiff-necked way, stubbornly refusing to die, regardless of the short-term public relations gain that would ensue.

Israel is a land of startling paradoxes. Its foremost satirist, Ephraim Kishon, director of the movie, *Sallah,* and author of the film, *The Big Dig,* has lovingly summed up his country thusly:

"Israel is a country so tiny that there is no room to write its name on the map of the world.

"It is the only country in the world which is financed by taxpayers abroad.

"It is a country where mothers learn the mother tongue from their sons.

"It is a country where one writes Hebrew, reads English, and speaks Yiddish.

"It is a country where everybody has the right to speak his mind, but there is no law forcing anyone to listen.

"It is the most enlightened country in the world, thanks to the Arabs.

"It is a country of elections, but no choice.

"It is a country where nobody wants to work, so they build a new town in three days and go idle the rest of the week.

"It is a country where nobody expects miracles, but everybody takes them for granted.

"It is a country whose survival is permanently endangered, and yet its inhabitants' ulcers are caused by the upstairs neighbors.

"It is a country where every human being is a soldier, and every soldier is a human being.

"It is the only country in which I could live. It is my country."

QUIZ

A. TRUE OR FALSE

1. An Israeli WASP is a White Ashkenazi Sabra with Pro-texion (connections).
2. Pitta is a Jewish puberty rite.
3. Golda Meir is the Grandma Moses of Israel.
4. A hora is a reformed nafkeh.
5. The leading Japanese convert to Judaism in Israel is the exiled Jewish princess, Taka Metziah.
6. There is no such thing in Israel as a kosher elevator, you're putting me on.
7. A brith is an abbreviated Jewish ritual which is the result of ineffectual birth control.

B. MULTIPLE CHOICE

1. Hatikvah is
    a) A Jewish chastity belt
    b) A herniated ulcer
    c) The Jewish Defense League
    d) The Israeli national anthem

2. Aliyah is
    a) Chief of the Arab Fatah
    b) Fat chef at Camp Kadimah
    c) Aramaic for "Go fall on your head!"
    d) Going to live in Israel

3. Kallah is
    a) A Jewish bride
    b) A twisted bread
    c) What's Jewish about the Andromeda Strain?
    d) A religious conference which winds up with the question: Where do we go from here?
    e) Arabic for my killa is your gedillah

4. The Ah-ha experience is
    a) Getting on the speaker's list is like making a reservation at an anti-Semitic hotel four months in advance

        b) When the disaster you confidently predict actually happens

        c) After two free drinks and a fine dinner, they pass out the UJA pledge cards

5. A kinahora is a) A bad eye

        b) When your kin dances the hora

        c) Jewish machismo

        d) A Jewish jihad

        e) A good eye

        f) What you shouldn't give your worst enemy

You get ten points for each true or false answer, six for each multiple choice. The correct answers can be found written in Hebrew (from left to right) on a swarthy bus boy with sideburns down to his Adam's apple in the Dairy Room of the King David Hotel in Jerusalem. Happy hunting!

CHAPTER TEN

HOW TO RAISE HIM TO BE A RABBI

The ideal solution to the problem of Harold is, of course, to induce him to become a rabbi. There are a few rabbis who are also in flight against Jewish life (some insist on being called reverend *doctor* rather than rabbi, and a few have abandoned the pulpit for the stock market), but they are exceptional. Most rabbis are dedicated teachers and preachers of Judaism. It is a high and noble calling, an opportunity for moral leadership and human service. Don't imagine that your boy will get a "call" or see a vision like a flash of revelation in the middle of the night. That's for Christians. If he gets a flash in the night, it's from salami and pickles after the late show. And don't think you can give him a *smicha* (ordination) intravenously.

There are ways to lead him gently to a decision to enter the rabbinate:

The first is to *oppose* his becoming a rabbi. If he raises the question, snort: "What kind of a job is *that* for a Jewish boy?" Drop a word here and there about the difficulty of the rabbinate, the relatively low pay, the idealism which is required to endure the demands. Tell him a good Jewish boy should go into his father's business, make money, contribute to philanthropy, endow a building at Brandeis or Tel Aviv University, live in Beverly Hills and raise a good Jewish family. Also, tell him that only a *nar* (fool) will devote his life to religion and, if *he* has *charisma*, you have *ESP*. Your son will then denounce you as a "fascist fink"; condemn your "corrupt, middle-class values" and fly out of the house, slamming doors, without walking the dog (who is not even Jewish). That is a very good first step.

The next rule is to join a temple where the rabbi is a swinger and a rebel. If you make the wrong choice and end up with an all-rightnik rabbi in a smug, all-rightnik temple, your plot will collapse like a South American government without American arms. No, the rabbi must be a dissenter, an iconoclast and—of course—a thorn in the side of his congregants . . . including you. He must be the type who afflicts the comfortable rather than the type who comforts the afflicted. He should be a prophet, not a priest. When you locate him, join quickly—he may not survive long. Read the temple bulletin and be sure to shlepp your son on those Friday evenings when the rabbi calls for the impeachment of Agnew, preaches on "What's So Hot About Virginity?", makes a non-negotiable demand of $10 billion in reparations from Christian churches for the suffering they have inflicted on Jews throughout the ages, and declares, "Thou art the man," while pointing at the vice-president of the synagogue during a sermon on "Exploiting and Castrating the Poor." Your son will sit there wide-eyed, while you and the other congregants groan louder and louder like a posse of constipated cougars.

On the way home, you and your wife will ream out the rabbi, skewer his sermon and impeach his motives. On cue, your wife will say: "If that man is a rabbi, I'm Racquel Welch!" And you should add your dulcet baritone to the duet: "I will see to it that that character is bounced right out of the temple! When did *he* ever meet a payroll anyway?" At which point, if you are lucky, your son will exclaim: "If he goes, I go! He's too good for you bourgeois businessmen. He's beautiful—and I'll fight you right to the wall!"

"Listen, son," you reply, "if you can't say something *bad* about the rabbi, don't say anything!"

Now have the swinging rabbi suggest to your son that he attend a Jewish summer camp conducted by the national movement. He will explain that he (the rabbi) will be on the faculty of the camp, and that he knows your son will enjoy the creative and stimulating program. When your son comes home and says he's thinking about going, knock it: "If that kooky rabbi is on the faculty, it's probably a training ground for free love, pot and anarchists! You stay home and help out at my factory; you'll be better off." So he'll go to camp.

Camp may provide the clincher. Indeed, a majority of the young men who currently enter the rabbinate have been turned on by the exhilaration of Jewish youth camps. It may well happen to Harold. The camp setting is exquisitely beautiful— mountains, lake, formal gardens, artsy-craftsy, the whole bit. The spirit is positively Jewish—and contagious. Religious services are held at the outdoor chapel overlooking the shimmering lake under God's own canopy. The program is creative, democratic and some of it is fashioned by the youngsters themselves. By controlled manipulation, the faculty, suffering bad cases of campitis, stay up all night to write the original Chasidic service which the kids next day will think they wrote. By controlled spontaneity, the kids explode into Chasidic dance and singing when the service is over, unless it is followed by a Quaker service of ten minutes of un-Jewish silent meditation.

The faculty is made up of rabbis in Bermuda shorts, sideburns, peace buttons, and beards, who are still young, although they may be over thirty. The program is intellectually alive. It connects Jewish values to the real issues of our time—war and peace, the sex revolution, the drug scene, campus unrest, black power, civil disobedience. He learns the Hebrew language and Jewish history, which he had artfully dodged during ten years of religious school. To Harold—and to the others—it is an eye-opening, inspiring, poignant and loving experience. For the first time, he feels that Judaism is both fun and meaningful. He sees Jewish teachings as values to live by. Well, if this is what it's really about, why not devote one's life to professional leadership of this vital way of life? In short, why not become a rabbi? The question is planted in Harold's heart like a tender seedling to be nurtured by the warmth and beauty of a deep personal experience.

Harold may be getting hooked already. For a year he will be the "house youth" at the temple, singing "zoom golly golly" for the tearful titillation of the Sisterhood. In his emotional response to the camp experience, he doesn't realize he is flourishing in a hothouse environment, light-years removed from his own—or any other—synagogue. He has identified the rabbinate with a very precious—and atypical—experience. The camp atmosphere is Jewishly buoyant, but it is connected to the real world only by the thinnest of umbilical chords. Harold, exalted, doesn't realize this. Don't tell him.

The spirit of camp won't last. The bubble will be burst by the cold contact with reality the first time Harold goes to services without a tie and is sat upon by the chairman of the Ritual Committee. Soon Harold, disillusioned, will be thrashing about, looking for a new value system. He will read Hermann Hesse and conclude that man has the "spirit of becoming" within him. He will read Lainge and conclude that the whole world displays schizophrenic tendencies. He will read Gurdjieff and see the unreality of life and the emptiness of the conventional wisdom. He will be cleared and processed in Scientology. He will be eating a piece of liver while reading *Portnoy's Complaint* and will become a vegetarian. Harold will set out on the voyage of life to discover his own soul. He will join a nudist colony, seeking the naked truth, but he will quit when it is clear that, as the first Jew in the colony, he is a visible sensation and distraction. He will briefly take up astrology and mainline horoscopes. In California he will spend two months trying to break into the sensivity circle, learning to touch, wallowing in the mud and crying. He will try LSD and take a bad trip to Acapulco. By this time, it will be clear to him that he has not yet unscrambled the mystery of life, and he will ask you for money to journey to India to join an exotic Eastern sect in the Himalayas. Let him go.

Harold will spend six months with his head shaved (which is already progress, don't knock it), wearing nothing but a silly grin, a beard and a loincloth, meditating in silence by the week, vibrating hopefully and eating wild rice and cheese kreplach. He will study at the feet of Mimeo Masharok, the exalted guru of the ancient East. Mimeo is a wizened gnome of a man. Each day they will sit in total silence, communicating with each other and communing with nature. At night they will watch Johnny Carson. Every two weeks, Harold will go out in the woods on safari, hunting the ultimate truth. In accordance with the sacred ritual of the sect, he will write down all of his sexual fantasies to bring back to Mimeo (on mimeo paper), who will read them silently while softly and inscrutably chuckling away and chanting his ooms. For a while, mysticism will seem to renew Harold's spirit. Then, one day, he will be ready.

He will turn to the guru and say: "Master, you have not yet spoken to me. Tell me, what is the meaning of life?" The guru will pick some lint from his belly button, smile quizzically, survey the vast sweep of the Himalayas and cackle: "Aylu v'aylu divre elohim chayim." Harold will say: "Is that Indian or Chinese?" "It is Hebrew," the guru will reply. "Did you not hear it from right to left?" "Hebrew? What does it mean?" The guru will say: "It means *these* and *those* may be the words of the Living God." "Yes, I understand," Harold will say, "but how do *you* know Hebrew? I am Jewish, but I didn't know *you* were Jewish. You don't LOOK Jewish!" The guru will laugh uproariously: "Chochum, of course I knew *you* were Jewish. All the kinderlach who comes here hung up about ultimate truth are Jewish. What other mishugoyim go to the mountains when they're nervous? WHY DO YOU THINK I WASTED SIX MONTHS SITTING HERE WITH YOU LIKE A GOD-DAM ZOMBIE? I'm a free-lance recruiter for the Jewish Union Seminary with branches in Cincinnati, Los Angeles, New York and Jerusalem."

And so, finally, you will have maneuvered Harold into the rabbinical school. For five years, Harold will become steeped in Talmud, theology, Torah, liturgy, homiletics and Hebrew. (History used to be taught but there was a historectomy after student protests about past-oriented courses, during which the seminary students demonstrated with placards: "The world teeters and the seminary peters!") The function of the seminary is to transmit the classical Jewish heritage and teach him words like *weltenschaung* (spelling it is for the doctorate). The job of the student is to absorb it like cotton batting. He will also learn how to speak in orotund, pear-shaped tones when preaching on "The Universe and Related Matters." He will learn how to stroke a platitude until it purrs like a pussycat. He will learn the do's and don'ts of the American synagogue. (*Do* go with the big hitters!) He will study the Halachah (Jewish law) to learn how to bend it to the exigencies of daily life. For five years he will be pickled in Jewish knowledge, at a cost of $25,000; is Harold worth it? He will pray daily, inserting the earplugs only when one of his classmates is about to inflict a practice sermon (a little soggy from the soaking and with notes scribbled in the margin: "Yell like hell here—content weak!") upon the student body. He will experience that terrible pain of the undelivered sermon. In his spare time, he will sit around the bumming room, possuk-hunting or reading *Playboy* or planning to put the hand of his sleeping roommate in warm water, awakening the faculty Arab scholar with the muezzin's Arabic prayer chant at 3 A.M., or Frenching the bed of the Homiletics professor who, at eighty, is the young Turk of the faculty. To help support himself through the seminary, he will spend two days a week as a student rabbi in Keokuk, Iowa—one day conducting Sabbath services, one day avoiding nubile single females whom the congregants strew about him like confetti.

(Some student rabbis make good use of standard books of "Great Sermons." One of the best and most serviceable sermons was one entitled "I Am a Hebrew," a brilliant allegory about the damp prophet Jonah. A small Southern congregation wrote to the seminary: "We again would like to engage a student rabbi for our bi-weekly, but do you by any chance have one who doesn't preach "I Am a Hebrew?"")

It will be, in short, the greatest education a Jewish boy can get, deepening his spiritual resources, quickening his frisbee, plumbing his talent, sharpening his sensitivities, stretching his horizons, doing everything—in fact—except equipping him to be the rabbi of a congregation. ("Rabbi, you mean the seminary didn't teach you how to work the dimmers?")

Throughout his career your son, the rabbi, will be envied and esteemed by his fellow rabbis not only for his scholarship, his erudition, and his achievements—but even more for the memorability and audacity of the pranks he perpetrated at the seminary in the good old days. Over the years the line between truth and fiction, *midrash* and apocrypha, will blur. This is known as the Oral Tradition. Nobody will know—or care—any longer whether Harold really arranged for a classmate at the seminary to officiate at the fake funeral of a stranger and that when the frightened young student rabbi completed the eulogy of the "dearly departed" and called upon the congregation to rise, Harold rose too, right out of the rented coffin, a blazing cigar in his mouth, driving his officiating classmate out of his wits as well as out of the seminary? True or false, Harold will

always be known, nostalgically and respectfully, to his classmates as "the Coffin Kid," a mark of undying respect. Indeed,
that event will ruin funerals for every one of his classmates. Not
one of them will ever again officiate at a funeral without fully
expressing the standard three G's for obsequies: Glance downward to the coffin for farewell and reassurance. Glance outward
into the crowd in consolation. Glance upward to heaven in
wry thanksgiving that good old Coffin Kid, preacher and
teacher, is far, far away preaching and teaching so that the
prospect of his popping up unexpectedly again, like a piece of
challah out of a smoking toaster, is as dim as an adolescent
memory.

And wasn't Harold the one to whom the beloved professor
Rev. Dr. Yates Hurrah said: "And tell me, mister, when did
you last look up Appolonius' 'Golden Ass'?" As for Harold's
legendary response, there are seven schools of thought with
seven versions equally apocryphal and in equally bad taste.

And so, culminating your fondest dreams, he will be ordained
a rabbi in Israel, a servant of the Jewish people, a teacher and
preacher of Judaism (saying: "And God said, and I quote . . .").
Who knows how many souls he will save for Judaism in his
career? Nobody. But, at least he will have saved one, the one
you were most concerned about—his.

CHAPTER ELEVEN

HOW TO RAISE HIM TO BE A JEWISH
BUREAUCRAT

Maybe you won't be able to make a rabbi of your child
(or vice versa). But don't despair. Perhaps, failing that, you
can get your son or daughter into a career of non-rabbinic
Jewish professional service. The Jewish community maintains
an astonishing network of organizations and agencies to meet
a multitude of needs: family service, mental health, aid to
Israel, service to immigrants, hospitals, aid to the blind, community relations, recreation, vocational service, education, welfare and religion. Tens of thousands of laymen serve the Jewish
community—and the broader community—in professional ca-
pacities through these agencies. By and large, these agencies,
after which many of the non-sectarian and Red Feather agencies
are patterned, attract superior personnel. For the most part,
however, there are no clear standards or training programs to
get into these fields. ("Son, human relations is not a profession, it's an ART. Either you've got it or you haven't. If
you've got it, flaunt it!") So let's try to get your Lennie or
Laurie to become a Jewish bureaucrat.

Here are some helpful tips:

1. Let Lennie or Laurie become a researcher. One of the
"in" things is research-and-destroy teams. The object is not to
provide *answers* but to raise the right *questions* (including:
"Where are we *going*? Where do we *want* to go? Why don't we
go there? And how much will the traffic *bear* for this study?")
as to the ills of the organization. Any one of the organization's

previous bureaucrats could *tell* you in five minutes what is
wrong, but to give *legitimacy* to these questions, it is necessary
to have the *hechsher* (seal of approval) of a bright-eyed and
prestigious outside agency, preferably a university like Harvard,
MIT, or Columbia. In addition, it is necessary to: a) Hire a
research "manager" who is good at subcontraction and who
refers to himself as "one" ("one would hypothesize"). b) Spend
$100,000 for a pilot project to prove you're serious. c) Go in
for sensitivity training and laboratory confrontation (which are
mod forms to conceal and collectivize the failures of psychological therapy). d) Produce a gobbledygooky report so bulky
it will be weighed instead of studied, which is a good thing
too because a real analysis would blow down the whole fragile
structure of the organization.

An example of good eclectic research was the finding of one
search-and-destroy team that, since studies show that the Israeli kibbutz raises the IQ of deprived Yemenite youngsters,
and children educated on Long Island do better than do children
in Appalachian schools, and Jewish children score higher than
Christian children even in the same environments, all children
regardless of race, religion or previous condition of servitude
should now be assigned to a pilot kibbutz of Jewish families on
Long Island. Another research team studied what makes a congregation tick without exploding. Still another examined: Is
there an inverse relation between the age of the sisterhood
president and the age of the rabbi?

Research is imperative because if you don't know where
you're going, any route will take you there. Researchers are
gamblers in futures. Thanks to research, the organization
(known to researchers as a "volog" which means voluntary organization) can start from aleph (in the beginning), give the
appearance of asking the unthinkable questions ("one thinks
so anyway"), rock the boat without changing the crew or
course, give employment to bright-eyed researchers, stir up
adrenalin and sleeping constituents, all the while secure in the
knowledge that no organization ever goes gently to the glue
factory (they merely change their rationale because they'd
rather switch than die) and, if torn apart by researchers gone
amok, divides, amoebalike, into at least three separate but
duplicating agencies, all desperately in need of annual injections
of therapeutic research.

One must not create the naysaying impression that research never leads to *tachlit* (brass tacks). Research frequently leads to plugging the research process into the program of the organization being researched. The most common recommendation of research is: create a "think tank" for long-range planning. This has now become a big business—think tanks are now being manufactured in a pilot project by an enterprising Jewish firm in Santa Barbara, which once had an exclusive with Robert Hutchins, but now supplies Jewish and ecumaniacal agencies as well.

A large Jewish religious organization, researched to death over the past twenty years, now has eight (count them) gurgling think tanks of its own lined up in a row, each containing a scholarly and charismatic rabbi seated within it, dynamically reading the Talmud to extrapolate the relevance of the Jewish tradition to modern problems. Each rabbi is daily fed inputs and data in interoffice envelopes, while the sister organization, happily impervious to the need for research, says no tanks. But why only rabbis? Couldn't your Laurie or Lennie occupy a think tank?

The really creative researchers do not merely raise questions —they construct GAMES. The master at this is, of course, Herman Kahn, but one can adapt the Kahn game to his own organizational purpose. (Joshua Shell has a game too.) What one must do is come on strong with an easel (easel come, easel go), a flip chart, and a magic marker. As one slashes a diagram on the sheet, one must tear it off and throw it on the floor before they can read it, thus avoiding unnecessary confusion. The trick is to stand in a sea of flip sheets while on one foot and talking off the top of your head, involving the people in a real-life game like, say,

> A—How many Jews in your town?
> B—How many non-Jews?
> C—Do you NEED that many non-Jews?

or

National

Regional   Board

Local Units

Why are the arteries of communication slogged? Are the arteries hardened? Why don't they answer our mail? What is a circular file? If national is the heart of our process, do we need: a) A transplant? b) Open-heart surgery? c) A new head? d) To move to the suburbs, near good schools? e) Should CBS take over the American synagogue? f) Others?

The most popular game is *relevance* which means the organization has to be where it's at and where it's happening or we're nowhere or out of sight. Why do rabbinical students have to know "E" from "J" in Talmudic tracts? What's *relevant* about *that?* Why study the prophet Jeremiah unless we can know where and when he will appear, standing on one foot, to talk to a conscientious objector today or a Black Panther tomorrow? What is the relevance of the temple fertility rites to the young chick who says: "I don't need advice, I take the pill!" Why have a Passover Seder unless we can turn it into a demonstration for Soviet Jewry, a moratorium vigil, or, when we say, "Let all who are hungry come and eat," the door will open and admit, instead of the prophet Elijah, the Salvation Army, drums pounding, with fifty hungry derelicts from the Bowery? *Relevance* is a good game, but it is rapidly becoming irrelevant as three thousand rabbis beat it into the *bima* every Sabbath. Relevance, like sex, is dead. It's already been replaced by "community."

Another game is NUMBERS (and it has nothing to do with Deuteronomy). This is played in every synagogue, every national denominational office, every organization. The spokesman says: Why are we obsessed with *numbers?* Who cares how many *members* we have? Why must we sink to the lowest common *denominator?* Why not *quality* instead of *quantity?* What's with this unseemly *competition* with other institutions? Judaism will not survive by the *numbers*—but only by the commitment of the few, the saving remnant, don't you know. Why must we play the ignoble *numbers* game, setting false goals for success? Why not lift our sights to the mountains, whence our strength comes? This game is great fun, gratifying the latent elitism of every member who thinks it is the OTHER members who make up the lowest common denominator and drag down our standards. Nothing, of course, is ever done to shuck off surplus members (except for non-payment of dues three years running), and the *numbers* game proves so much more *relevant* than constant talk about *relevance* that it invariably INCREASES the *number* of members on our roster, which is a damn good thing, too, because a continuing deficit is the name of the REAL agenda that the leaders of the organization have to wrestle with while everybody else is playing GAMES and fiddling with flip charts.

Still another good game is the WHITHERS. It is best played at conventions, but is also good for sermons, conferences, dialogues, and symposia. Just ask: *Whither* our Youth? *Whither* Judaism? *Whither* Israel? *Whither* the Diaspora? *Whither* the synagogue? *Whither* God? After you have whithered away both the subject and the audience, you can switch to futuristic whithering, like: *Whither* American Jewry in the year 2000? *Whither* the Jewish Defense League in 1984? Futuristic whithering is highly recommended because it turns their attention to the Great Beyond so that they will not notice that we are gurgling down the drain Here and Now, despite the stirring sixty-minute speech by the researchers on the importance of NONVERBAL or McLuhanesque Communication!

2. Youth. The best opportunity for the young person who wants to be a Jewish bureaucrat and doesn't qualify as a researcher ("no third degree") is to become the "inhouse youth" (which is classier than the "outhouse youth") on the staff of a national agency. Every organization needs such a youth counselor to try: a) to translate "childrenese" into English for the adults; b) to establish a liaison with young people to wean them to our organization; c) to line up the youth, the favorite *object* of the researchers.

The prognosis for success in this job is about the same as for the president of a university (they are both no-win jobs), but, if Lennie gets the position at twenty-five, he will only have to hang on for five years, after which he will be thirty and over the hill as a youth liaison and maybe he can get a job with the ADL (Anti-Defamation League), infiltrating the JDL (Jewish Defense League).

To be a Jewish bureaucrat, Lennie will have to be able to cope with kids (always to be referred to as "young people" or "our future leaders"). The youth bit may soon pass away, but it is *de rigeur* now. No Jewish organization can ignore it. Some time ago the imperative was Christians. Interfaith was in; Christian leaders had to be invited to every meeting to tell us they loved us. Then interfaith escalated into ecumania, we all got worn out, and Christians were out unless they would join us in denouncing "Christian silence" loud and clear. With blacks, it was the same thing. First, we needed blacks as evidence of our own liberalism. But, after a while, some blacks refused to be pussycats and began to roar like lions (which ruined Jewish conventions, which had always been places where the lambs pass resolutions not to attack the lions), and we found it was more satisfying to talk about race relations without blacks present. Likewise, with youth. Today we need them. Tomorrow they may be as superfluous as yesterday's Brotherhood Dinner. But, meanwhile . . .

It is vital for the young bureaucrat to know how to "involve" younger people in the organization, especially, as it is said, in the "decision-making process." After all, our youth are the FUTURE. They are the leaders of *tomorrow*—that is, if they don't abandon us *today*. How do we do it? The best way is to pre-empt them and co-opt them as the poverty program does with militants, and as this short-sighted organization has done with Lennie. Short of that, however, if we fail to co-opt them, we should study them as if we are Margaret Mead and they are pre-Columbians and "exhibit" them. There are a few hopeful directions:

A. Don't risk "involving" them in something slogging, dull or typical. For example, don't invite them to an ordinary event of a lodge, chapter, or circle or to a routine religious service at the temple. They'll register ennui. Instead, invite them to put on their own creative service which will include a multimedia Johnson's Wax movie, strobe lights, a Dave Brubeck jazz festival, a simulated pogrom, seven minutes of Quaker silence, and a dozen youngsters sitting barefoot on the pulpit, strumming guitars and talking in tongues while the parents sit in their pews in horrified revulsion, afraid to open their mouths lest the youngsters notice and become alienated, pow, right in the middle of the service.

B. Lennie shouldn't try to train, guide or prepare the younger people for participation in adult Jewish organized life. Just throw them in. The important thing is to baptize them into an event which will turn them *on*, not off. Like, say, an international conference in Jerusalem on Jewish education. I mean, why should only educators get to boondoggle? Why not their victims as well? It's only fair. If a foundation of some sort picks up the tab, it will serve as a further incentive for the non-co-opted youngster to go to the conference where, at an appropriate moment (probably when table grapes looking suspiciously California are served in the fruit cup), he can rise up, denounce materialism, boondoggling, affluence and the terrible waste of money and time at such international gab fests. Not having a youth rebel or two in your delegation to prove you are tuned in is as old hat as having a large Madison Avenue firm without a black vice-president in the window.

C. Or, failing something as swinging as an international conference, or a tour of the Soviet Union to study the condition of the Jews there, Lennie could invite him to your organization's national convention at the Century Plaza in Los Angeles (electric blanket for every delegate), Fairmont in San Francisco, Roosevelt in New Orleans or Fontainebleau in Miami Beach. Make sure all the other local groups also bring a youngster or two as part of their delegations; why should Lennie's group be the only one to suffer? On the way down in the plane, the youngsters will demand Lennie give them the power of attorney to scrutinize the "investment portfolio" of the temple to make sure that not one penny goes to benefit South Africa, Spain, Poland, Greece, Laird, or Dow Chemical. Lennie mustn't tell them the temple has no portfolio—only some bank notes totaling $200,000 in accumulated debts. They know an Establishment cop-out when they see it, even at 20,000 feet. In sizing us up, and seeing right through us, the kids go on the correct premise that there is less there than meets the eye.

D. Now the youngsters (average age sixteen) have descended on the convention, seeking each other out, like generational lemmings. We didn't merely invite them as *individuals*; we want them to be a "youth presence," a force in the movement, all of which has an effect on the youngsters analogous to showing pornography to Portnoy. Set aside the loveliest room in the hotel—would you believe the Robespierre Room?—as their youth caucus center where they can eat cake, sing and dance, and plan a bloodless coup d'état against the *ancien regime* (meaning Lennie).

E. Shepp nachos from the youth. Observe them moving into the Resolutions Committee and all the interstices of the convention like Elmer's Glue. Note how well informed they are; they have done their homework. Don't be intimidated when the youngsters get up to the mike and denounce the lavish vulgarity of the hotel; applaud wildly when they suggest that henceforth we meet in the woods; how can we talk about peace in the Boom Boom Room of the Fontainebleau, and, by the way, have we examined the hotel's table grapes, investment portfolio, and racial composition? Smother them with agreement. By the third day of the convention, the kids will have occupied all the mikes, submitted their non-negotiable demands, and gained overwhelming votes on every major issue. ("I mean, you want me to vote against them and lose our youth?") Lennie and the adult delegates will watch in fascinated horror, wondering where will they strike next, and congratulating each other on your flexibility and openness, hailing the "youthful ferment" in the organization, oblivious to the warning of Winston Churchill that he did not become Prime Minister to preside over the liquidation of his own empire.

All grownups, including Lennie, will have to squirm and wince a lot because the kids will denounce their "silence" if they just sit there, and if they say something, the kids will zing whatever they say as "hypocritical and weasel-worded," (which is better than "bullshit"). But what choice is there? No youth, no relevance. No youth, no future. Obviously, if the convention were enjoyable (as in the old days), it would be proof positive of its decadence. In the olden days a delegate could sit down at a business session and adopt a resolution against the pollution of the environment—and feel good about it. No more. Now he's got to listen to the technical testimony of a sixteen-year-old *mavin* on ecological environment, who has a built-in crap-detector, who knows more about the subject than all the senior delegates put together, and who wipes all the A.K.'s out by concluding "how ludicrous for this split-level community with the buttoned-down minds to be passing a resolution on pollution while you sit here befouling nature's atmosphere with a thousand stinking cigars, which burn, baby, burn!"

Our adult anxiety about our youngsters gives them a powerful weapon against us. Either we "listen" to the voices of the young, or they will "abandon" us. This gives them the whip hand. They can intimidate us with the tyranny of the young. In the olden days, you could have said: "Look, son, have you ever met a payroll?" But, as Lennie fully understands, you can't try it with the NOW generation.

One large adult Jewish organization overdid the "youth presence" bit, went to such lengths to welcome young people into the decision-making processes of the organization ("we would be proud to entrust this movement into the hands of our youngsters") that the kids executed a coup d'état and installed a seventeen-year-old pimple-faced lad as president of the B'nai B'rith lodge. (His issue was that by making Hayakawa "Man of the Year," the lodge had sacrificed its soul.) By the time the B'nai B'rithniks began to suspect they had gone too far ("we thought *we* could use *them*"), the young president had put through a constitutional by-law limiting the membership to persons under thirty, thus provoking the national ADL into a public retort that "discrimination on account of age is no less repugnant than discrimination on account of race and religion."

The seventeen-year-old swept into office on an anti-Establishment platform: No banquets (use the money for the poor and for Jewish education which is also poor), no conventions (meet in the woods, be real), no fund-raising projects (let's set our priorities straight), replace synagogues with coffeehouses, no more awards. (Anybody who is in this for the *koved* is not worth honoring anyway.) Within months he saw that the lodge was dissolving before his eyes; *he* became an Establishment fink. In his first annual presidential address, he warned about the "excesses of youth," complained that most young people "had not read the minutes of the last meeting," pointed to the danger of being tyrannized by the young, and closed with this peroration: "To a member who has something to contribute—everything. To one who demands attention just because he has acne—nothing. We shall not sign a blank check for anyone, old or young. Besides, what do *they want* anyway?"

3. HOW TO MOVE THROUGH THE CHAIRS.

Once Lennie has insinuated himself into the bureaucracy, the trick is to endure meetings (which are dull, but better than working) and to "move through the chairs," which is how he shimmies up the greasy pole of a hierarchy and develops shiny pants. Jewish agencies pay relatively low salaries (except for top fund raisers who say: People give to *people,* not causes), but they compensate with titles and hats. Anybody worth his salt wears at least three hats—director of this, associate director of that, consultant to this, etc.—as well as shiny pants. These titles mean little in one's own agency, but they look great on a curriculum *vitae* (and the hats look groovy in a Turkish bath) when he looks for his next job. "Moving through the chairs" is the process of gaining through attrition, rising through the table of organization by doing nothing that antagonizes his superiors or the laymen. For some, this means doing nothing. An axiom is that only busy people have time for additional tasks, so if Lennie's not busy, he won't have to do anything, particularly if he is the kind of bureaucrat who can always be relied on to come up with a good reason not to do something.

There are a few sure-fire ways to become a competent bureaucrat. One is to read the New York *Times* each day from stem to stern; the *Times* is the daily bible of Jewish life. Lennie will have to know the portion of the day. It's the source and authority for almost everything he'll say and hear that day. It prints the good news, the bad news, and the Agnews. The real pros not only read the *Times,* they CLIP it. A few carry special scissors in their pockets at all times so they can cut up the *Times* on the subway, the New Haven, or airplanes. When Lennie reaches his office, he'll ask his secretary to Xerox five copies of the clippings. What to do with the five copies is a challenge inasmuch as every other pro in the agency has clipped the same items and THEIR secretaries have also Xeroxed five copies each. Most of these Xeroxed items will wander about the office in interoffice envelopes for a month, ultimately finding their way into the "files," which, since they have been centralized for greater efficiency throughout the agency, are harmlessly lost in the catacombs of the warehouse in New Jersey.

In most large agencies it is difficult to distinguish between executives and secretaries. In general, the executives are men and get the salaries and the titles; the secretaries are women and do the work. (Some follow the Biblical injunction: "Where there are no *men*, be *thou* a man!") The more capable the secretary, the better the executive looks—and the more superfluous he is.

In the old days, a boss would dictate a letter, the secretary would type it, show it to him for approval and signature. No more. Now the secretary reads the boss's mail (which consists largely of memos written by other secretaries in the names of *their* executives) before he arrives at his desk, full of lame excuses for being late; she writes the reply in his name, forges his signature and mails it out. (If he wears more than one hat, she may have to *answer* her own letter too.) One agency executive was on sabbatical for four months before his secretary discovered his absence. She terrorized him into returning from Israel to take her to lunch for her birthday. Another executive was dead for two years before his lay board found out about it. (They put a belated obit notice in the *Times*: "We will never forget the invocation he delivered at our last biennial convention.")

One of the largest Jewish agencies had an independent efficiency study, which recommended pensioning off all executives who had earned less than three Kiddush Cups and frankly acknowledging the power of the female Rasputins who pull the strings from behind their smoking typewriters. The agency grapevine picked up the threat immediately, and executives quickly worked up a tenure plan—for themselves—just in the nick of time.

Lennie should beware of the Peter Principle, which has been brilliantly described by Dr. Laurence J. Peter and Raymond Hull, and which is at work in the Jewish as in all other bureaucracies—and which means that everybody rises to the level of his own incompetency. He should stay in his own chair if the next empty chair would take him out of the invisibility of the proofreading department into the fish bowl of public relations or think-tanking. Promoting from within looks democratic but it is often suicidal.

To make it in the Jewish bureaucracy, Lennie will also have

to learn how to talk shorthand, distribute Kibbudim (institutional patronage), hold the layman's hand, and "field the questions." The latter can be his Achilles' heel as can a big mouth. He must learn to open a meeting by saying: "Shall we go around the room?" He'll jet around the country like a grasshopper, dropping out of the sky to buzz his local chapters in Los Angeles (particularly in January), Atlanta, Peoria, and Buffalo (never in January). He must learn never to count the house, because people don't go to meetings when the weather is good and also when the weather is bad. When he finishes his pitch on "Whither Jewish Youth?" (why so *long*? When he asked what he should speak about, they TOLD him about twenty minutes!) the Chairman will invite questions. This is it. They didn't hear a word of his pitch as they were grinding their mental axes for this moment of truth. He'd best be ready. He should tread water. Each question will open with the gentle dripping of acid: "You people up in headquarters in New York City . . ."

One question will *always* be: "Your speech was very nice, and this is the third time I've been stimulated this week, but where do we go from here?" Another will be a slashing ten-minute denunciation of the national office for wasting the local's dues and presuming to "speak for me." The Chairman will interrupt and say: "Sam, please, that's not a QUESTION, it's a *speech*. What's your QUESTION?" Sam, glowering, will say: "Can't I raise my question in the form of an answer?" Lennie must be able to field these bouncers without a bobble. He can't be a Dr. Strangelove. He must always preface his response with: "THAT is a very good question" or "I am grateful to you for bringing that up" and, immediately thereafter, do a verbal quickstep, a graceful waltz and a fast pirouette, throwing rhetorical dust in the air, and spinning right out the side door into a waiting car and out of town, thus eliminating any incipient threat of violence or, worse, organizational schism.

YOU GIVE ME THE JEWISH ANSWER;
I'LL GIVE YOU THE JEWISH QUESTION

To be a Jewish bureaucrat, you have to know a Jewish Answer to a Jewish Question. You also have to know a Jewish Question to a Jewish Answer. So let's play A and Q:

Answer: Nothing.

Question: What does it mean when the speaker removes his watch and places it on the lectern?

Answer: If you don't strike oil in twenty minutes, stop boring!

Question: How long should I speak?

Answer: Who doesn't?

Question: Who speaks for American Jewry?

Answer: He doesn't want to be a rabbi; he wants to be a temple president!

Question: Rabbi, my twelve-year-old son wants to be a rabbi. He wants to know what you do when you're not preaching?

Answer: I was good, my audience was bad.

Question: How was your speech?

Answer: It's a business doing pleasure with them.

Question: Rabbi, do you and the rabbetzin have to go to every bar mitzvah party?

Answer: Smith.

Question: How do you spell your name again?

Answer: The sooner the better.

Question: I'm glad you felt my sermon was good and superfluous, dear. Do you think I should publish it posthumously?

Answer: Up yours.

Question: Tell me, Sam, what should I do if both of my vice-presidents up their voluntary dues?

Answer: I'm not a used-religion salesman!

Question: Tell me, Rabbi, did you ever have to meet a payroll?

CHAPTER TWELVE

HOW TO PREPARE HIM FOR A CAREER

Okay, your son didn't make it as a rabbi (His feelings were hurt when the professor said: "You know approximately as much Bible as Balaam's ass,") and muffed his chance to become a Jewish bureaucrat. (He could never learn the clichés—he mastered "nitty gritty," "nuts and bolts," "devil's advocate" and "finalize," but could never tame "rubric," "hang-up," "bottom line," "track record," "shopping list," "gut feeling," or "inputs.") But there are plenty of other jobs for a good Jewish boy.

The generational progression of your family may be prototypical:

> Great-great-grandfather—peddler
> Great-grandfather—junk
> Grandfather—steel
> Father—metallurgy

Melvin may revert to being a peddler (of posters, buttons, and underground papers) unless you can crank him up and point him toward a Jewish career, whatever that is, lest he continue with his Horatio Alger in reverse.

In the old days, Jews used to place the highest value on piety, learning, and good deeds. So, naturally, sages and scholars and saints were at the summit of the Jewish pecking order. Jewish tradition esteemed the making of a life, not just the making of a living. Both the life of the mind and the sweat of honest physical labor were reverenced in Jewish history. Thus, some of

the great rabbis made their livelihood through the simple work
of their hands—as cobblers, carpenters, blacksmiths, farmers.

Today everything is *tomer farkert* (Yiddish for upside down).
Sandy Koufax, Art Shamsky, Paul Newman, John Lindsay and
Moshe Dayan are at the summit; athletes, actors, politicians,
and effete snobs are among our heroes. And go find a rabbi with
mechanical aptitude! (Well, there is *one!* He gave a paper at a
rabbinic conference on "A Modern View of the Eternal Light"
which his colleagues flocked to hear and steal from, but it
turned out to be flip-chart diagrams on how to transistorize the
Eternal Light so it would chime the "Hatikvah" on Israel's
anniversary. Most rabbis can play golf, but, in the Rube Goldberg mechanical aptitude tests, they fall somewhere between
small girls and baby chimpanzees.)

In our time, Jews still produce sages and scholars (we're
light on saints lately, let's face it)—but they are, usually, sages
of chemistry, law, government, sociology, journalism, or social
work. Thus, the Jewish value system has been transvalued—
Americanized, Westernized, secularized, homogenized, and
bowdlerized. All this shows up in contemporary Jewish vocational patterns which demonstrate radical shifts (and some
shiftless radicals also). Is there really a discernible pattern of
Jewish employment choices? What kind of a pattern can your
Melvin run? And who should I say is asking?

What are the cultural characteristics which shape the pattern
of Jewish vocation? Who knows? Yet, there are such values,
including the following,* and you could look it up:

1/ *Independence.* Jews tend toward occupations where
they are free to do their own thing. They prefer occupations where they are able to make their own choices and
decisions. Melvin's present occupation is meditation, but
it's just a stage. General Electric and Bell Telephone
are nice corporations, but General Dayan doesn't have
so many partners!

2/ *Mobility.* A Jew tends to want to be his own boss, as
much as possible, as to where, with whom and how he
works. If he doesn't like it, he likes to be free to range,

* I am indebted to Rabbi Richard J. Israel, Director, Hillel Foundation,
Yale University, for this information outlined in his article in *Dimensions*,
Summer, 1969.

like a Marlboro man. He doesn't like to be riveted to a certain place or company. He wants to be portable, like television, mobile like gas, and he wants to be able to move ahead, in the words of Casey Stengel, "slow but fast."

3/ *Association with other Jews.* It is not necessary for most of his coworkers to be Jewish. But, on the other hand, the place mustn't be *Judenrein* where Melvin is the "house Jew," Exhibit A of a WASP establishment's liberalism. There is an element of security—and safety—in numbers. A very successful Jewish man, climbing through the chairs of a large non-Jewish brokerage firm, found himself adopting protective coloration—reading the *Daily News,* registering Republican, keeping a low silhouette at the office, having three martinis for lunch, and joining a country club he despised. Finally, when he heard himself making anti-Semitic comments, he threw over the good salary to go into business for himself where he is now poor but happy, independent, mobile, etc.

4/ *Urban environment.* Jews have been, for centuries, urban animals. They still are. Urbania includes suburbia but it doesn't include Little Falls, Minnesota; Provo, Utah; Potemkin Village, Nebraska; or the Everglades. A Jew in rural America is like a Jewish segregationist—either a fish out of water or the local Babbitt. Generally a Jewish person wants access to theater, good music, a synagogue and the amenities of modern civilization. He doesn't have to use them, he just feels more comfortable knowing they are there. Jews eventually felt safer in the anonymity of city life, but this may be changing as the city increasingly takes on the menacing quality of the Roman Coliseum.

5/ *Intellect.* By and large, Jews prefer jobs that require brains to jobs that require physical aptitude. A young Jewish lad in St. Paul got a job as an assistant in a filling station. In a week, he misplaced eighteen gas caps, damaged two cars so badly they had to be taken to the back yard and shot, and he drowned an open-roofed Peugeot in 350 gallons of oil when he turned the wrong knob on the hydraulic lift. But during the week he endured this debacle, he conceived the idea of the "Hello,

I am _____ " tags to be plastered upon convention
delegates and also composed an imperishable dirty lim-
erick which can still be read on the wall of the men's room
of the Lowry Hotel. *Gam zula tova.* It goes to show.

6/ *Status.* For most Jews, a satisfying job with high status
is more important than money. This explains why Ben
Gurion resigned his job as Prime Minister to become a
shepherd in a kibbutz in the desert.

Add all these characteristics together and they spell DOCTOR!
These values *do* affect Jewish vocational choices. Honest.
Medicine probably fulfills these requirements more than any
other profession. It provides independence, status, mobility,
authority (how did *that* get in here; it wasn't listed above),
portability. As a bonus, one can have his masochistic impulses
stroked by membership in the AMA, which is the medical
version of Robin Hood and his merry men, though it is pretty
awkward for a nice Jewish boy to be working for the Blue Cross.

But even within the field of medicine, there are choices.
Should Melvin go into internal medicine, psychiatry, surgery
or orthopedics? What's Jewish about that choice? Plenty. After
all, the psychiatrist works alone (except for one patient who
shouldn't even be lying there, his hour has already lasted fifty-
one minutes). So does the internist. On the other hand, the
orthopedist and the surgeon are part of a team (you can't tell
the doctor without a score card) and who needs this collec-
tivism? So, while the world prizes the surgeon over sturgeon, the
Jewish medical world gives higher status to the internist and
the diagnostician who live by their kops and not by their hands.

If Jewish boys become doctors ("MY son, the doctor, is
drowning"), shouldn't Jewish girls become nurses? The answer
is an emphatic NO! Nursing is also a team operation, like
playing for the Mets. A nurse is constantly taking orders, guff,
supervision and bedpans. Also, the hours are brutal, it's not
very portable, you use your hands more than your kop and it
does not easily satisfy the needs of personal fulfillment. A Jewish
girl should get married. And if she wants to marry a Jewish
doctor, the hospital is not the place for it. Be a patient instead
("You have acute angina, dear." "I know, doctor, but what
about my heart?"), especially at the Concord.

Jews tend to move into theoretical fields more frequently

than experimental. The Jewish scientist seems to prefer a situation where he has a study, a blackboard, a piece of chalk, a nosh and a problem to solve rather than a situation where he is a part of a large group, requires vast equipment, has to raise his hand to get the floor, and ends up one of twenty anonymous scientists who publish a report. Here, too, the thrust for individuality seems to affect Jewish professional choices.

This Jewish hang-up about individuality is even more conspicuous in music than in medicine or physics. Jews tend to become violinists and pianists rather than wood-wind and brass players. Did you ever hear of a Jewish mother who gave her child woodwind lessons? Did you give Melvin wind sprints or violin lessons, which? The proof of the pudding is that the Israeli Philharmonic, a first-class orchestra, has an excellent string section but the orchestra has to import non-Jews from far and wide to fill the wind-instrument section. There are not enough Jews to play these instruments. So it is clear that violins and pianos are Jewish instruments but brasses and woodwinds are goyish. Can you name a famous Jewish flutist or French-horn player? The piano and violin are launching pads for Jewish youngsters to shoot for the stars. If they fail, they can always give music lessons to the next generation of Jewish youngsters. This doesn't apply to Melvin who pawned his violin to buy a knothole ticket to the ballpark.

Outer space has become a world-wide obsession, but the Jewish obsession has always been inner space. Jews flock to those fields of psychology where they can learn about themselves, other human beings, and the nature of man and society. Karl Menninger wrote an essay entitled "The Genius of the Jew in Psychiatry." He saw the Jew as the explorer of the human condition, a kind of roving astronaut of the psyche, a person peculiarly equipped to empathize with the pain of others. Thus it is that so many American psychiatrists are Jewish. This may stem from the Jewish tradition of being able to look at all sides.

The story is told of the two men who came to the rabbi to mediate their bitter quarrel. When the first petitioner completed his case, the rabbi said: "You are right." When the contending petitioner presented a diametrically opposed case, the rabbi said: "You are right." Exasperated, the rabbi's wife ex-

ploded: "But how can you say they are both right?" Replied
the rabbi: "And you are right, too, my dear." That rabbi, not
Freud, was the real precursor of the modern psychoanalyst who
can sit there silently while a patient writes a whole book and
then say: "And now may we begin?"

Now that you understand the topography, social dynamics
and etymology of Jewish occupational choices, you are ready to
guide Melvin into a professional career. Remember that Jewish
family life is the rock on which he stands and behind every
successful Jewish man is an amazed mother-in-law. Actually,
Melvin doesn't want to do any of the nutty things described
above. He couldn't care less about the statistics and would like
to repeal the Jewish law of averages.

So buy Melvin an out-house on a farm in the foothills of the
Berkshires. There are many advantages. Economically he could
probably support himself, being handsomely paid by the government (like Senator Eastland) not to plant cotton. If this
doesn't meet his budget, he can also not plant potatoes and not
raise pigs (which will make *bobbe* happy). Also, Jews may be
urban animals, but Melvin can commune with nature, raise a
little cain and barley, sow wild oats and experiment with curds
and whey. Socially, it is advantageous also. He can bring all of
his freaky friends and start a hip kibbutz, a way station to
Israel (see Chapter Nine). The final advantage is the most
important. He will be at least three hours away from you, which
all by itself, will add to your life span the 7.2 years which
those crummy cigarettes have stolen away!

And now that you have some idea what Melvin will do when
he grows up, what will *you* do when Melvin grows up? Raising
Melvin is a parental obligation and challenge; but what will
you do with yourself *after*? Start all over again with *his* children,
seeking to repeat your disasters into the next generation? Don't.
Go find *yourself!* . . .

And yet, for the individual, these vocational patterns mean
nothing. A Jewish person can well become a jockey, a window
cleaner, a herring mavin, a clam digger, or a cop. Take Asa
Dybbuk, for example. Asa Dybbuk was a tough, hard-nosed
Jewish kid, who grew up in the rough streets of Brownsville,
and became one of New York City's finest. The police force
was dominated by the Irish Mafia, but Asa never sought to

conceal his pride in his own Jewish identity. He was an officer of the Shomrim, the organization of Jewish policemen. This earned him the grudging respect of the Irish cops, most of whom were fallen Catholics whose cars had the plastic Jesus on the dash, a decal of the American flag in the window, and "Keep Christ in Christmas" and "Support Your Local Police" bumper stickers. In fact, his fellow officers were so impressed with Asa's Jewish loyalty—Asa was also an active supporter of a small Orthodox shule, and carried his twelve-year-old boy by his ears to Sabbath services every Saturday morning—that they dubbed him "The Rabbi."

That casual circumstance, in the end, changed Asa's life. It happened this way. The massive crime wave of the late sixties terrified New York City, shook its political foundations, and challenged the police to new techniques to cope with runaway crime. Asa was shifted from the precinct station, and, along with thousands of his fellow officers, assigned to the streets, disguised to blend easily into the various neighborhoods of the city. Asa was, alternately, a Good Humor man, a lady of the streets, a litter basket, a blind umpire, a doctor who doesn't make house calls, an Arab missionary, Spiro Agnew, a swish mailman, and a Greek bearing gifts at a local gift shoppe.

Then the crime statistics zoomed out of sight in the Jewish Chasidic neighborhood of Williamsburgh (Brooklyn), and, naturally, somebody thought of disguising a platoon of cops as Chasidic rabbis. Also, naturally, somebody at headquarters said: "A-ha, how about Asa the Rabbi?"

So Asa Dybbuk, the cop, grew a beard and *payess* (his twelve-year-old son began to call him "my father, the hippie rabbi"), and was dressed up in a long, flowing black kaftan, a *streimel* (black velvet hat), *tzitzis* (the strings at the end of the *tallis*, prayer shawl) and all the accouterments of the ultra-Orthodox believer. Under his kaftan, he carried a gun, a knife, a walkie-talkie, a police whistle, and a Bible, as contingency equipment. On his very first day, he was mugged while buying a copy of the *Forward*, and he decked four hoodlums with four artfully placed karate chops. Immediately, word whistled through the grapevine. The Fighting Rav became an instant hero. "Who is he?" asked a local chasid. "Who knows?" responded another. "God sent him, like Judah Maccabee, to pro-

PREPARING HIM FOR A CAREER

tect us against our enemies. Don't ask too many questions."
And so Asa was dubbed Judah the Second. Disciples formed
about him. As he walked the streets, he was thronged by the
admiring devout. He felt mildly guilty impersonating a spiritual
leader and exploiting the gullibility of the pious, but crime
declined in the neighborhood—and that was his assignment,
after all.

Asa's superiors had arranged for him to take a small flat
in the decaying neighborhood to increase his credibility. But,
amazingly, his flat became a religious center, like ancient Sura
or Pumbedita. Scholars came to thumb the Talmud and to
argue about *pilpul* (small points of law). Youngsters came,
admiration shining in their eyes, to watch the Fighting Rav,
Judah the Second, eat his meal. Some chassidim came to ask
the Rav *sheilahs* (questions) of *halacha* (Jewish Law). Example: "Rav, naturally we do not permit such pagan things as
television in our house. But my son has somehow, God forbid,
become a zealot for the New York Mets, sneaking away to
waste hours every day in ignorance. Mets—Shmets, this is a
business for a nice Jewish boy, particularly one who is en-
joined by the tradition: An ignorant person cannot be pious?
So tell me, Rav, shall I beat him?"

Asa scratched his beard and said: "The Ribono Shel Olom
wants Kavanah (the spirit), and sometimes it must be admitted there is more genuine prayer going on inside Shea Stadium than in the heart of one who calls himself pious. So
when the Mets beat the Astros, you can beat your son!"

The scholars would lift their eyebrows at the Rav's unortho-
dox responses to the "sheilahs" ("Are you sure he's not a damn
Reformer?" scoffed one cynic), but the proof of the pudding
is in the eating. And, since the policewoman at the station
house daily filled his flat with good pudding, not to mention
absolutely kosher gefilte fish, knadlach, and herrings, Judah the
Second quickly became the informal leader of the community.
He loved his work, but he was getting too fat to fit into the
kaftan, and besides, he was up night after night intoxicated
with the ecstatic singing and dancing—that wild joy of life—
which is the glory of Chasidism. After a week, he began to
weaken, muttering: "It's easier to give traffic tickets, or bust

college kids, or fight muggers than to be the Fighting Rabbi of Williamsburgh. God forgive me, I need a little sleep!"

Asa was undone by his own success. The Fighting Rabbi began to be honored by the Jewish community of New York City. Almost every night he was the guest of honor at another banquet. The Jewish War Veterans placqued him for "demonstrating that muscle and spirit are interwoven in the Jewish soul." The Jewish Defense League, presenting him with a pair of brass knuckles and a David sling mounted on a baseball bat against a field of blue and white, feted him at their karate camp for "reviving the spirit of the Maccabees and Bar Kockba, thus demonstrating that we Jews will not be patsies any longer." The Zionists got into the act, honoring Rabbi Judah the Second for "bringing to the streets of Williamsburgh the self-respecting courage, the dignity of assertive self-defense which animates our people in Israel, that bulwark of democracy in the Middle East."

Finally, the great rebbes of Williamsburgh gathered at Asa's flat to bestow upon him their highest distinction—to make him the Chief Rav, first among first. Deeply moved, Asa almost choked on his gefilte fish. As one by one the distinguished rabbis rose to extol his virtues in Hebrew and Yiddish, speaking from right to left, Asa began to feel the heavy weight of guilt. What had he done? Why had he allowed this harmless masquerade to reach this point? How could he deceive these loving, pious, and God-fearing people, flesh of his flesh, bone of his bone? Such deception was itself a crime, a *chillul hashem*, a profanation of His name. And, besides, with all this eating and dancing and no sleep, he would not survive much longer anyway. Also, Asa knew that he was about to be exposed in any event. Time was running out. In the front row were young radical students from Brooklyn College, hissing: "Pig! He's a Pig!" As the rabbis rose in unison to applaud him, Asa decided to blow the whistle on himself.

He reached inside his kaftan and blew the whistle. Instantly, the flat was bursting with Good Humor men, ladies of the streets, blind umpires, litter baskets, homosexual mailmen, Spiro Agnews, Arab missionaries, Greeks bearing gifts, as well as the hissing students from Brooklyn College who had come to tear off his cover and humiliate him. "I can pretend no longer,"

Asa said softly. "I cannot continue to trespass upon your trust. You see, my beloved rebbes, I am not only not worthy to be the first among you, I am not worthy to be in your midst at all. In the language of the young people present, my dear rabbis, I must tell it to you like it is. I have been putting you on. . . ."

"*Vus zugt ehr?*" one Rabbi asked his neighbor. ("What is he saying?")

"Oink!" shouted Brooklyn College. "You're a *Pig!*"

"A PIG? YOU SHOULD FALL ON YOUR HEAD!"

"A PIG? YOUR MOUTH SHOULD TURN TO TREFE!"

"A PIG? VAY IS MEER! YOU SHOULD CATCH CHOLERA!"

"A PIG? THAT'S FUNNY, YOU DON'T LOOK PIGGISH!"

"OINK! THE RABBI IS A PIG. HO, HO, HO CHI MINH! THE RABBI IS A PIG!" shouted Brooklyn College.

ENDING NO. 1

"Yes," Asa said. "It is true. I am a policeman—a pig, a nobody. But do you know why I am here. To arrest God, that is why! Our people have never yielded all authority to God. He has His responsibilities; we have ours. He judges us; but we judge Him, too. Did not Abraham argue with God, demanding that the Judge of all the world should be merciful? Did not Job contend with Him through all his suffering? Did not many of our sages defy Him and accuse Him? Ribono Shel Olom, Ruler of the Universe, I am a simple policeman, a nonentity, but you are the Policeman of the Universe, and I know there will always be crimes of stealing and fighting and lying and killing and war among men so long as some men diet and others go hungry, so long as men cannot share a stranger's pain, so long as justice and peace are denied. And so, dear God, with deep reverence and awe, because I am an unworthy man, a humble person, I charge you with being man's accomplice in failing to build your Kingdom here on earth."

There was a gasp, a shocked sucking in of air, and then an incredulous silence, broken after two eternal minutes, by one of the rebbes: "Asa Dybbuk, for such unutterable audacity, such chutzpah, there are only two possible responses. One is to place you in charem and hoist and shackle you like the animal you profess to have been; but why should we make you a Jewish martyr? The other is to acknowledge your prophetic fervor and give you *smicha* (ordination) on the spot! We have decided to grant you your smicha, intravenously, and ordain you a rabbi in Israel."

And so the good pious people of Williamsburgh can be seen studying at the feet of a zealous young rabbi ("We may have lost a fighting cop but we have gained a spiritual kop, *l'havdil*") or, out on the quiet streets, exercising their Dybbuk.

ENDING NO. 2

And, then, a strange sepulchral voice, which sounded as if it were filtered through a think tank: "Look who is trying to become a nobody! In the words of the sage, Casey Stengel, in commenting on the miracle of the Mets, you have come on slow but fast, Asa, you name-dropper you!"

ENDING NO. 3

"Yes, I am a pig—a cop. I confess—I have deceived you. Forgive me!" said Asa.

Asa raised his hands in supplication: "*Ribono Shel Olom.* God of the Universe. For my sin in deceiving my people, forgive me. For masquerading as a sage when I am only a lowly *am ha'aretz* (ignoramus), forgive me. For degrading faith into a mere means to a civic end, forgive me. But, dear God, could I have done these things if you, the Policeman of the Universe, had not wanted me to? Therefore, you, Ribono Shel Olom, are my copartner, my accomplice. It is for *you*, not the Police Commissioner, that I have done what I have done. And it is with you that any complaints should be lodged! Why don't you answer me?"

A voice, muffled and sepulchral, said: "Because you're such a nudnick, that's why."

ENDING NO. 4

And so, Asa Dybbuk the pig turned chicken at the moment of truth and decided to stop horsing around and take it on the lam. Muttering "bull," he dived out the window and ran away, taking refuge in Jake Orwell's Animal Farm, living as a hunted beast, wanted by the New York Police Department (one rabbi AWOL), wanted by Brooklyn College, which has burned him in effigy, and unwanted by the Williamsburgh Chasidim who have placed him in charem as a fake messiah and would just love to deposit him at the glue factory.

ENDING NO. 5

"Yes," Asa said, "I am a pig—a cop. I have indeed put you on—forgive me." Asa put his hand to his face and pulled off his false beard, removed his wig to reveal a crew-cut haircut, and took off his kaftan and stood there in his jockey shorts, holster and undershirt emblazoned with the seal of the Police Benevolent Association. The clean-shaven square picture was so repellent to Chasidim and Brooklyn College both that they fought down their nausea and, turning their back on him, they slowly filed out of the room, leaving Asa crushed and alone like a plucked chicken or exposed pig. "Look," mumbled Asa to himself, "nobody's perfect."

ENDING NO. 6

Ending 6 is to be written by you, the reader, in one hundred words or less. If ending 6 is better than the above endings, nobody (including Doubleday) will be surprised and it will be printed in full in the second printing (which we doubt—Doubleday) of this volume, we should live so long, and so dangerously, unfortunately without credit because as it has been said by whatchmacallit: "Originality is a pair of sore eyes." If anybody has a suggestion for the rest of the story (or book), who asked you?

CHAPTER THIRTEEN

HOW TO MARRY HIM (OR HER) OFF AT A JEWISH WEDDING

You haven't really lived until you've been part of a Jewish wedding—either as one of the leading actors, a bit player, an extra, or just plain *nochas-shepper* (pleasure-taker). In the life cycle of the Jew, the wedding is the climatic moment, for which all else has been prelude. When a Jew wishes another Jew the deepest possible fulfillment, he says: "Next year, we should see your daughter (or son) under the chuppah (marriage canopy)." The central message of the wedding, as it is of Judaism itself, is embodied in the toast: *l'chayyim*, to life!

The Jewish people has a gift for family. Mark Twain paid tribute to the warm solidarity which marks the Jewish family. The Jewish divorce rate is low (but growing), and most indices of family instability—alcoholism, delinquency, etc.—show Jewish families more stable than any other group except the Chinese. The close Jewish family is legendary despite the effort of big mouths like Philip Roth to portray or portnoy it as a catastrophe. You can take the Jewish mother, as Roth does, and place her wiggling under a microscope, like a bug, but yet the Jewish family endures as a fortress against danger, a transmission belt of Jewish values, a launching pad for life, even if maybe also a training ground for assorted hang-ups as well.

Some historians believe that the concept of family is one of the most humanizing contributions which Jews have made to civilization. The nature of Jewish family life stems from the historic Jewish conception of marriage as *kiddushin*, a sacrament. Judaism didn't see marriage as Christianity did—a concession to the weakness of the flesh, or as a device purely for procreation. Judaism has never put down sexuality. Judaism cherished it as an expression of man's creativity. Sex is not seen in Judaism as a nasty little secret or as a grudging indulgence to the dark side of our nature. It is seen, joyously, as a gift from God. An unmarried person is regarded, by the tradition, as an unfulfilled person. (About an unmarried rabbi, *neboch*, you shouldn't even ask.) This exalted concept of marriage has invested the wedding ceremony with deep emotional overtones.

This sense of kiddushin (holiness) fills the Jewish wedding with a special aura. The Jewish wedding, as it was observed in the Eastern Europe of *Fiddler on the Roof*, has been described thusly in *Life Is With People*: "A wedding is the most joyous and most elaborate festivity in *shtetl* (ed: the Jewish village of Eastern Europe) life. It represents the fulfillment of the individual, who becomes fully adult only when he marries. . . . It is the archetype of all festivity and rejoicing—the symbol of joy and completion. The Sabbath is a "bride"; an especially successful celebration is "as merry as a wedding"; one who is called up to read the last section on Simchas Torah is a "bridegroom of the Torah," and one who reads the beginning of the new first chapter, starting the new round for the year, is the "bridegroom of in-the-beginning."

Thus even secular Jews, whose Jewishness consists of going to Jewish weddings, bar mitzvahs, and funerals, rarely repair to a justice of the peace to perform the marriage. They go to a rabbi. The rabbi, invariably, meets with the eager couple in his study for a series of premarital conversations which deal with making a Jewish home, raising a family (2.7 siblings), home observance, the importance of the synagogue, etc. These conversations also range, increasingly, into the area of sexual and psychological adjustments (this may or may not be helpful to the young couple, but it sure makes the rabbi's day more interesting) in building a sound marital relationship. If one of the pair is non-Jewish, the rabbi will probably refuse to officiate unless the non-Jewish partner converts to Judaism, and the convert is usually a more zealous Jew than the one who came by it naturally.

Jewish parents feel strongly about their children marrying
Jewish. Even parents whose Jewish knowledge and commit-
ments to things Jewish are *shvack* (weak) have a tendency to
go up in smoke when their child announces an intention to
marry a non-Jew. Is this tribalism and bigotry, as the young
often believe? Is this a Jewish emulation of Catholic rigidity?
Maybe, but it is more likely an unerring instinct for survival
—the kind of instinct which has made it possible for the tiny
Jewish people to endure three thousand years of solicitude at the
hands of the Gentile world.

So how can you prepare yourself to cope with the fact that
interreligious marriage is increasing among Jews and it may
be your son who marries out of the faith? The classic Jewish
parental response is: Darling, don't worry about me, I'm a
modern parent, you go ahead and marry the girl, I'll just go
upstairs, and cut my throat. Cynics have also suggested that it
would be a good idea if your son would date a black girl in
college (in the halcyon integration days, Jewish girls used to
wife light-skinned Negro civil rights leaders, who later became
fierce advocates of black nationalism and denounced whitey
from pillar to post) so that when he switches to the blond,
blue-eyed shiksa he met in Anarchy 109, you'll be quite relieved. And when his chosen partner burrows like a mole into
Jewish literature (I mean, do YOU know who A. D. Gordon
was?) and takes to the conversion course like Golda Meir to
diplomacy, lights the candles for Shabbos and becomes a *far-
brente* Zionist, you'll *shepp nochas* (pleasure) and ask your mate
why your *shmendrick* (fool) of a son can't be as Jewish as
your daughter-in-law.

Actually, despite the Jewish nervousness about intermarriage,
it may turn out that intermarriage is a secret bonanza for Jews.
The transfusions may be exceeding the leakage. The net total
of conversions and children raised as Jews may outnumber
any loss. Studies show that more Jewish men than Jewish women
intermarry. Why? Who knows? One prominent sociologist, who
also doesn't know, Dr. Leonard Fein, puts it this way. "So the
significant question is: Are these women simply spinsters
bereft by renegade spouses, or shrews, who were unmarriageable?
Many of them don't look shrewish!"

Dr. Fein suggests that "the only solution would be to de-

crease the number of Jewish men who intermarry or urge these
ladies to intermarry, or have a program of planned promiscuity."
Heavens to Betsy! Such thinking may be fine for Fein, who is
a big man on campus, but it does not sound so great in Great
Neck and shakes up a lot of people in Shaker Heights, Ohio.

Statistics also show that in America nowadays one bride out
of three is pregnant! So if you have three daughters, marry off
the first two and then beat the stuffings out of the third who
doesn't *look* pregnant (or shrewish for that matter). Similarly,
one of every four children born in America is Roman Catholic.
So don't let anybody tell you it is anti-Catholic to drop birth
control pills into the orange juice of your married daughters
after they (and the pregnant old maid) have produced three
kids each! As Harry Golden says, only in America!!

The Jewish wedding itself is a moving and touching event.
The guests arrive at the synagogue or the hotel at the appointed
hour. The ceremony begins promptly half an hour later. (One
family, prompted by a compulsive rabbi, announced that the
wedding would begin "Promptly" at the appointed hour, but
the printer was too offended to print it.) The guests divide
themselves automatically into the kallah's (bride's) side of the
family and the chossen's (groom's) side. The center aisle becomes a kind of Berlin Wall. Later, at the wedding party, every
conversation will begin, cautiously: "Which side are you on?"
One couple recently, fearing a bad overmatch, insisted on choos-
ing up sides all over again before the kickoff so that the teams
would be more nearly equal.

Now the music begins. The organist belts "Lohengrin"
(what's *Jewish* about "Lohengrin" anyway?) and a relative
(which side is she ON?) sounding like a female Nelson Eddy,
sings: "I Love You Truly." Then, the processional begins. The
rabbi, the grandparents, the groom, the bridesmaids, the best
man (grandmother really thinks *he* is the best man, all things
considered including the groom), followed by the radiant bride.
Now the handkerchiefs billow on both sides of the wall like
sails at the Larchmont Regatta. The couple joins hands and
stands before the rabbi under the chuppah, a lovely flowered
canopy, and the tender wedding ceremony takes place.

There is more crying per capita at a Jewish wedding than at
any ethnic function, including the Irish wake, the Greek bap-

tism, the Chinese laundry, or the French kiss. Why is this? A
Harris Poll (taken by Abe Harris of Toledo at his niece's
wedding) revealed that 37 per cent were crying because they
thought of the end of innocence and the sweet vulnerability
of the youngsters. Thirty-five per cent cried for themselves,
lamenting the death of youth and the slow decay of childhood dreams. Ten per cent cried to keep up with the Cohens.
Four per cent cried because the beloved zayda, whom everybody revered, couldn't be at the wedding. Two per cent cried
because the bobbe, a peppery termagant, WAS there, muttering in her gravelly *sotto voce* Yiddish, so that it bounced off
the back rows, "so why does she have to marry such a shlemiel
(fool)" and "if *this* is a *rabbi*, I'm Tiny Tim."

But all this, of course, was before the winds of change came
huffing through the youth generation and rippling the chuppah
and all other Jewish institutions. When politics, the family,
universities, public schools, and the law are all being restructured
before our unbelieving eyes, we should not be surprised that
even so hallowed an institution as the Jewish wedding is likely
to be scrambled in the youth revolt.

A preview of coming attractions (bite your tongue) appeared
in real life in a New York City hotel in 1969. On the surface,
it was a typical Jewish wedding. Typical in every way—except
one; the bride and groom were SDS rebels from Columbia
University who had met during the occupation of Hamilton
Hall in the seizure of 1968. They agreed to the religious ceremony, under duress, he refusing to wear a tuxedo, consenting
only to blacken his sneakers, and she attired in a dashiki and
barefoot.

The rabbi, nearing the climax of the ceremony, asked the
young couple to repeat after him in Hebrew the ancient and
haunting vow: "Be thou consecrated unto me." The couple
had informed the rabbi in advance that they wanted to add an
original personal vow of their own. They did.

"I vow," said the bride, "to oppose this bourgeois, middle-
class hypocrisy. I agreed to have this ceremony perpetrated to
please my family, but I must protest against this counterrev-
olutionary mockery. How can we stand here in silence while
you marry us in accordance with the laws of New York State
while the Rockefellers and Fords are crushing the faces of the

poor in Harlem? What is the relevance of all this religious mumbo jumbo to the liberation struggle?"

"Right on," proclaimed the groom, holding up his fist, "and I vow to liberate us from this oppression. What is this nonsense anyway? We have been living together for ten months. Now all of a sudden we are man and wife? What the hell does New York State know? Query: Is marriage still relevant? Who wants to live in such an institution? And I protest this racist scene. Do you think there are any poor blacks or Puerto Ricans in the top management of this chintzy hotel? Why are the guests and the rabbi white and the waiters black? I'll bet they serve California grapes in the dining room! Marriage is a status-quo institution designed to domesticate youth, and we enter it under bitter protest. We reject your high-fidelity marriage code. We will love and honor so long as we groove together, and we will war against your tribal customs and your corrupt society. We are doing this only because we couldn't refuse her mother and my mother, but we want to tell you now loud and clear: UP AGAINST THE WALLS, MOTHERS!"

The rabbi, thereupon, cheerily concluded the ceremony and, afterward, everyone, including the bride and groom, danced a wicked hora. Everyone kissed the bride and got a little drunk and ate too much and, all in all, it was a very gay revolutionary simcha.

In 1969 Rabbi Shlomo Carlebach, wearing love beads and strumming a guitar, married a young Jewish couple in Golden Gate Park in San Francisco, under a canopy rigged to four bamboo poles before a wedding party of over one hundred beautiful people, many of them bearded, barefoot, and bemused. The couple had met in the rabbi's anti-Establishment temple, the House of Love and Prayer, where, according to the Ortho-dox rabbi, young Jews are "turned on" by the Chasidic joy and prayer of services which begin Friday at sundown and last until dawn. The hippie wedding consisted of three and a half hours of singing, dancing, storytelling, prayer, and mysticism under the canopy of heaven. It caused a gnashing of teeth and icy comment in the Jewish Establishment of San Francisco. However, reposts that the wedding party was stoned with stuffed dherma by disgruntled bay caterers have been stoutly denied.

Another couple insisted on being married under the sky in the Big Sur mountain. The wedding invitations instructed the guests to wear boots and contained a map telling them to turn left at the giant elm, advance to the shady side of the mountain, ford the stream, turn right at the cave and gather under the redwood. The bride's mother said, "Call this a wedding? It's like visiting my JNF trees in Israel. And I didn't lose a daughter—I gained a nothing!"

But, these are still aberrations. Most young people still go for the more conventional weddings. Query: Which table are you assigned to for the wedding party? This is a conundrum. Is it better to be close to the table where the wedding party sits? Does status reside in the low table numbers or high? What criteria go into the determination of which table you are assigned to? Are all the nudnicks confined to one table? Are the Republicans segregated with the old maid aunts? Did they keep a dossier on the people who got too juiced up at the bar mitzvah party eight years ago—and did they put these lushes as far as possible from the bar? Are the various branches of the family tree spread into different tables to make it easier to play FHB (Family Hold Back) if we run short of food? Did they put the heavy cigar smokers at one table so that they could sicken only each other and so that everyone else will have a fair crack when the cigar box is passed around and before the heavies wipe out the box? (The maitre de at one wedding announced: "The cigars are counted.") Or is it possible that the guests are assigned arbitrarily by pulling names from a hat or by a giant lottery? If so, why is the author always at table 34 which is right next to the men's lounge and at an impossible angle from which to get to the bar? This is not an accusation, just a question.

There is also the question of whether the reception should be kosher or non-kosher. Many traditional Jews observe the dietary laws (no mixing of milk and meat, absolute prohibition of certain foods, such as ham, lobster, pork, etc.), and any wedding these persons are associated with must be kosher-catered. (When a Jewish person describes the wedding as "religious" he usually means the food is kosher.) Also remember: the difference between Reform and Conservative Jews is that the latter expect their *rabbi* to keep kosher. Many non-

Orthodox Jews do not observe the dietary laws, and the question becomes a live one for their child's wedding. The solution is usually imposed by the grandparents, who are likely to be strict observers of *kashrut*; and, while they may in the end swallow the Reform rabbi provided he wears a yarmulke ("Even the Pope wears a nice yarmulke!"), they will choke before they will permit shrimp and bacon to corrupt their grandchild's wedding. I know a nice Jewish girl from a kosher home, who, when she became twenty-one, was grimly taken by her father to a restaurant to eat ham for the first time—a practice oddly analogous to the father taking his son to a bordello to usher him into manhood.

Whether kosher or non-kosher, the food will be plentiful, the dancing will be zesty, and at least four generations will join hands in a joyous and wild hora (Uncle Max will pull a groin muscle doing a mean gezotski inside the circle and will be waived out of the league), which will make the rafters sing and be glad, causing the groom to mutter to the bride: "I feel like we're the wedding scene at *Goodbye, Columbus*." Which injudicious comment, overheard by the bobbe, evokes the comment: "A klog (curse) on Portnoy and *Goodbye, Columbus* both!" and, *sotto voce* again, "Oy, with such a nice best man, leave it to her to marry this *yold* (fool)."

Which raises the most important point of all. Remember, it is your child, not you or your parents, who has to live with his (or her) mate. There is the wonderful story of the Jewish boy whose mother disapproved of every girl he brought home. Then, one day, he met the "right" girl—she LOOKED just like his mother, she TALKED like his mother, she THOUGHT like his mother. Elated, he rushed her home, and, sure enough, his mother LOVED the girl. The trouble was, of course, the father HATED her. It just goes to show you. It's really not your business. It's THEIR bed, and they have to lie in it. We can only hope that they will wait until AFTER their nice Jewish wedding. Meanwhile, mazel tov (congratulations) to you as the young ones go off to live in a psychedelic dungeon in a decaying neighborhood *your* parents moved away from fifty years ago, to fill their flat with the kinds of things her mother threw away as junk, and to honeymoon in countries your parents ran away from when this cockamamy century was still young!

CHAPTER FOURTEEN

HOW TO GET OFF THE POT AND, IF ALL ELSE FAILS, BAIL OUT

What should you do if you discover that Harold is smoking pot? You can't just sit there like a *jlob*. You have to do something. Perhaps if you had done something long ago, instead of sweeping the problem of drugs under the rugs, it would never have come to this. But now everything has hit the fan. What are you going to do about it? There are several possibilities, among which are the following:

1. CONTINUE TO SWEEP IT UNDER THE RUG. Although not recommended, there IS at least the virtue of consistency to this response. Let's say you are cleaning up your son's room (you mean, you haven't trained him to make his own bed *yet?*), a chore you have grumblingly held onto in order more easily to rifle his wastebasket and drawers for sequestered copies of *Playboy*, interesting letters, his diary, pornography and any other items on your embargo list. (When he catches you in the act, you indignantly make clear you are merely gathering up his dirty underwear.) But, lo, this time you find a couple of odd-shaped, funny-smelling cigarettes concealed in a tobacco pouch. Hear no evil, see no evil and spread no evil. Merely field strip the joints. Tear off the paper. Crumple the tobacco between your fingers. Drop the remains on the floor. Take a broom and SWEEP THE PROBLEM UNDER THE RUG. (This makes you a pusher, but at least it doesn't make Harold a pothead.)

2. QUIETLY TRY TO FIND OUT WHERE HE IS GETTING THE

DREAD STUFF. If he is getting it from one of his schoolmates, you can tell yourself (and your husband) that Harold has simply been influenced by pushy friends and by Dr. Spock, after which pack up the family in the middle of the night, lifting the sleeping Harold out of his bed and into the car, and move to the home of relatives in Potemkin Village, Nebraska. If, however, you find that Harold has been growing the stuff in your back yard or in the sunroom, you can say "it's just a stage," but you may have some horse of a different color.

3. KEEP YOUR COOL. Keep everything in perspective. Set your face in a mask as impassive as a Greek chorus. Tell yourself: I can tell you're upset because your hands are sweating, but leave us remember than anywhere from 30 to 60 per cent of America's young people have experimented with the weed, and how is that different from the silent majority boozing during Prohibition, or sleeping around in your youth? Besides, there is a crucial difference between occasional smoking and heavy use. So don't start fantasizing about poor you, why has he ruined your life, after all you have done for him, you'll have to kill yourself!

4. HIT HIM! You and/or your husband should have done this years ago—certainly when he was ten and tried to hijack the Good Humor truck, or the time he built a miniature ABM system and blew up the bathroom, and the time he mixed hashish into the turkey dressing, or the time he sold a/c-d/c batteries outside the convention hotel of the Mattachine Society! You have been altogether too permissive, drat Dr. Spock. Remember, the virus of non-violence, like charity, begins at home. Now he thinks he can get away with murder, which would never have happened if you had killed him a few times when he really needed it.

5. DO NOT ALLOW REPRISALS TO ESCALATE THE CONFLICT. Arrange a mutual non-aggression pact. Why should you and Harold mutcha each other so much? If the Russians and Americans, with their conflicting systems, can live and let live, why can't you and Harold? Coexistence is better than communication, and separate but equal is better on the nerves than trying to face up to your problem, especially if Harold is your problem, which we know by now is clearly the case.

6. TALK IT OUT! This is, of course, a last resort because it is

a no-win tactic. But, sometimes, it is unavoidable as, for example, when one day Harold says to you and your husband:
"Like, could I talk to you both?"

You and your husband file into his room, sheepishly, wondering what you did wrong this time, or is he just going to
give you another reading list?

"Like I hope you won't get, you know, uptight by what
I have to say to you both, but like I've been a little disap-
pointed in your behavior lately and, before it gets out of, you
know, hand, I thought we should have a little talk and maybe
I can see what seems to be, well, wrong with you both. Now,
I don't want to, like, chew you out or anything, you know, but
I do want to nip things in the bud like before you make things
even worse, you know. *Now*, do you know what you did?"

Silence.

"Okay," Harold said. "Who has been, like, spying on me
again? Which one of you burgled my room, it's supposed to be
private? I don't want to hassle with you. Just admit it and say
you're sorry and we'll forget all about it. Isn't that fair?"

Silence.

"Don't just stand there, like. What are you thinking about?"

Your husband speaks: "I'm thinking why the hell do your
mother and I have to feel guilty? How do you always manage
to reverse roles like this? What did WE do? Sure, Mom was in
your room and yes, she looked around, and it's a damn good
thing she did, too, because she found—"

"Like pot," Harold says blandly. "She found, you know, pot,
right? So?"

"WHADDAYAMEAN SO?" You find your voice. "You are
using *drugs*, Harold! *Drugs! Narcotics!* The last thing we ever
expected was to see our own son using *drugs. Why, Harold?*
Why, for God's sake? Your father breaks his back for you, but
we must have failed you somewhere."

"Aha, so you admit you were spying on me, turning my room
upside down like narcotics agents! Aren't you ashamed?"

"STOP THAT, HAROLD!" your husband exclaims. "YOU
are the one who should feel ashamed! Why do you twist everything upside down? It's YOU, not MOM, who broke the law!"

"Oh, come now, Dad," Harold says, "what did I really do
—I mean, like, existentially? I didn't hurt anyone. Grass gives

me an occasional lift—it, you know, relaxes me. Why do you two belt a cocktail before dinner and why do you drink at parties? You both smoke cigarettes—nicotine is worse than pot. So why are you, like, carrying on?"

"Don't give me THAT!" your husband storms. "Marijuana is illegal and you know it. Every day kids just like you—good kids, good families—are busted out of school, their pictures in the newspapers, their futures wrecked, their parents humiliated—"

"That's *it*, that's *it*," cries Harold. "It's YOURSELVES you're worried about, not me! Be honest. Be real. Like, man, no hypocrisy, no crap. Tell it like it is."

"HAROLD!" erupts your husband. "*Stop it!* Stop trying to put *us* in the criminal's dock!"

"Look, I haven't like killed anybody—not even you. I haven't raped anybody. What have I done that's so terrible? A smoke? A joint? I don't touch the, you know, hard stuff. Why must you adults be so hung-up? Why don't you just like call the cops and put me in, you know, jail for five years!"

"Show respect!" you sob. "It's not just the law, Harold. It's also YOU. Why do you NEED this stuff? It's a crutch! What weakness is there in you that needs crutching?"

"Listen," says Harold softly, "like stop crying already. Mom, you're always crying—you even cry at supermarket openings! But, I mean, after all, like, do you really know what you're talking about? Tell me, have either of you ever *tried*, you know, pot? Do you know the difference between pot and heroin? Your damn law doesn't!"

"Of course we haven't tried it!" you and your husband protest in unison.

"Wanna *try* it? Like wanna *turn on?*"

"No, dammit! Stop that kooky talk!" you exclaim.

"You know something, darling?" your husband says softly. "Of course, it's *wrong* and all, but maybe we should at least see what it's like, just once."

"*Stop that*, honey!" you cry. "It's *illegal*, it's *wrong* and you *know* it!"

"Oh, darling—just once, so we'll know what we're objecting to. I mean, after all, what could happen? Why should we, like, take somebody else's, you know, say-so?"

"Honey," you say, "now *you're* talking that way—everything's *like* and *you know!*"

"Come on, darling," your husband says. "As long as we've got all that stuff swept under the rug, let's try it once."

"Oh," you sigh doubtfully, "I suppose it wouldn't hurt to try it just once. But *not with Harold.* We're not going to do it *together,* Harold. You just leave one, like, *thing* here—and you leave the room and leave us like, you know, alone! . . . And Harold, when are you going to get a haircut?"

And, thus, you finally talked it out, frankly, with Harold—and what happened? What happened is that you and your husband got BUSTED, that's what happened! The cops finally let you go, with a warning and a lecture, which was terribly embarrassing but not as bad as the sneaking suspicion that it was Harold (who left a note: "I have gone to California; will be back in ten years") who had not only turned you ON, but *IN* as well! . . .

If life with your revolting youth has reached this pass, then the time has come to emulate your neighbors, the Ayn Kleinikeits—neighbors whom you love, in the Biblical sense, as much as you love yourselves which, in a confused time of self-doubt and generational conflict like this (as Ciardi says: "Whoever isn't confused these days isn't thinking clearly"), isn't very much. Somebody has said that if we really loved our neighbors like ourselves . . . we'd kill them. Anyway . . .

Mr. and Mrs. Ayn Kleinikeit had five children—three in college. Putting them through college was a strenuous financial and emotional burden, but Mr. Kleinikeit was a good gray executive for IBM and Mrs. Kleinikeit was in charge of dirty books at the public library and both Kleinikeits moonlighted and scrimped to carry the load. Came the summer vacation. All the children came home. Mr. and Mrs. Kleinikeit were delighted. It was a reunion they had anticipated all year long. The delight lasted until ten minutes after each kid landed at the airport. During the first week, their college daughter cried most of the time, while the boys slammed doors.

Then the oldest boy's girlfriend arrived from New Orleans and moved in. The oldest daughter's roommate from Sarah Lawrence telephoned from camp—she said it was a "drag" and she was splitting—and arrived to occupy the couch. The youngest son was an aspiring debater at the University of Wisconsin, and he was immensely pleased when the entire debating team (Resolved: Bring the war home, kill the parents) unexpectedly arrived and moved in. The youngest daughter, feeling left out, telephoned her neighborhood girlfriend and asked her to "sleep over." She rushed over with her toothbrush and stayed three weeks. Two complete strangers from Kansas City, walking by the house, felt the magnetic pull of community—and stayed ten days. Next, the telephone rang. Cousin Seth was back from Europe, he was at Kennedy Airport, and wanted to join the ingathering of the clan. He came, he saw the gathering kibbutz, and bedded down in the back yard in his sleeping bag. Before leaving for Europe, Seth had oscillated between two lovely neighborhood girls. Hearing of Seth's return, they both moved into the Kleinikeit household, occupying adjoining hammocks they strung up in the basement over the oil burner. Every available bed was assigned at four-hour intervals. No bed ever got cool.

There is a characteristically gentle sweetness with which today's young embrace each other. They don't, of course, extend it to the adults whose job it is to fix the meals, clean up after them, run the switchboard, and provide transportation. Soon, meals were being served by Mrs. Kleinikeit around the clock, like Stewart's Cafeteria. The washing machine and the dryer (and most of the youngsters) were constantly in heat. The dishwasher began to groan. So did Mrs. Kleinikeit, whose own bed was available to her only from 6 P.M. to 10 P.M. while the "gang" was night clamming at the beach. The Kleinikeits were pleased that their kids liked to be home, and that they were comfortable enough to bring their friends. And the spontaneous dropping in also appealed to them—the Kleinikeits were easygoing parents, and they prided themselves on their rapport with the young. Indeed, most nights they sat up all night with the youngsters, sitting cross-legged on the floor, while rock music blasted from the stereo, incense fumes drenched the air, and every conversation began with the word, "like . . ." and ended with "bullshit." But, when the young people at 3 A.M. suddenly leaped into getaway cars to go to the beach to watch the moon set, Mr. and Mrs. Kleinikeit were left in silence to pick up the glasses, dishes and overflowing ashtrays from the floor and clean up the inevitable mess. "The kids just don't get hung up on things like cleanliness, maybe they're right," they explained to each other glumly.

After three weeks, Mrs. Kleinikeit began to feel like an indentured slave. Her smile had become frozen, but inside she seethed: "They're exploiting me! They don't even see me! Those mouths never stop eating! Am I a rug for them to stomp on? I'm an *object*, not a *person!*" Mr. Kleinikeit had begun falling asleep at his office, his head on his desk, dreaming of an isloated and quiet island of sanctuary where infanticide is gently practiced. While his *machismo* friends had taken up golf and bowling and broads, he had (rather smugly) always insisted that his family was his joy and relaxation. And now, he hated to admit it—going home filled him with about as much anticipation as getting on the Long Island Railroad. To make matters worse, Mr. and Mrs. Kleinikeit had virtually stopped talking to each other. A long sullen silence began to stretch between them. Privately, each one blamed the other for having allowed the house to be invaded, infiltrated and occupied. Secretly, each one began to phantasize escape—solo escape! Each began to mutter to himself: Who needs the whole shmeer? The house, the family, the headachy music, the strange smells, the filth, the confusion, the barefeet, the pot, the mob scene? Oh, to be free, to get away from it all, to start again!

So, in the middle of the night (which by the youth clock comes at noon) while the masses were sleeping throughout the house, Mrs. Kleinikeit sneaked down the back stairs, knapsack over her shoulder, and tearfully began to scribble a farewell note. She was disturbed by a creaking on the front stairs. Aha, it was Mr. Kleinikeit, his bones creaking, a look of amazement on his face, a knapsack on HIS shoulder, irritated that he couldn't even find a pencil to write his getaway note. "You can't even find a pencil in this damn house, those cannibals must eat them," he muttered to her. That broke the ice. Mr. and Mrs. Kleinikeit, who hadn't spoken for three weeks, looked into each other's eyes, evoking the depth of understanding and love of twenty years of shared lives, joined hands, and slipped out the door together without a word—or a note.

The Kleinikeit house is still jumping, howling, and blasting, but Mr. and Mrs. Kleinikeit have run away. The kids have appealed to the police, left a description, put want-ads in the papers, and frantically telephoned all the Kleinikeit friends. "How can they be so irresponsible?" asks the oldest son. "Couldn't they at least call us up and tell us where they are, we shouldn't worry? If something was bothering them, couldn't they sit down and tell us, wouldn't we try to understand? Sometimes I just don't understand that older generation. What do they WANT anyway?" But, *gornisht holfen.* How do the children know that Mom and Dad, after grooving beaded and barefoot in Sausalito for six months, then living under the stars in a sleeping bag in an old catacomb in Rome, have now joined with thirty other runaway parents in a childless kibbutz called ENOVID in the Upper Galilee of Israel?

CHAPTER FIFTEEN

EPILOGUE

This book has been written with tongue in cheek. (I didn't have a pencil.) It pokes fun at everybody in sight—we adults, the kids, the universities, our hang-ups. And yet, obviously, beyond the laughter (which, frankly, sounded pretty *shvach* at times—what happened?), we are dealing with the most important questions of our time. And these are not laughing matters. (Tell me, was THAT your problem?) Obviously, also, these problems transcend Jews and Jewish youth. I have referred to my own group because the particular is the best symbol of the universal (and because I think Jews are like everybody else, only more so).

Remember, America is not a finished product, or a melting pot, you should pardon the expression. It is in constant motion, like the pieces of a kaleidoscope. You can't tell the players without a score card. What is happening now in swiftly changing patterns is that the blacks are becoming the Jews in American life, the Jews are becoming the WASH (White Anglo-Saxon Hebrews) goyim, and the youth are becoming the blacks. So watch as youth becomes the new hated minority, displacing blacks, and we have mounting backlash, harassment, and persecution against young people, especially the hairy and way-out types. So, to save time, the author is organizing a National Association for the Advancement of Young People (NAAYP) which will be leagued with the League Against Defamation of Youth (LADY), monitor all speeches by Vice-President Agnew, press for pro-youth civil rights legislation, and demand inte-

gration of a 20 per cent youth quota on all draft boards
and in the Joint Chiefs of Staff.

In all seriousness, I believe that young people in America
in our time have rendered a harsh—and essentially correct—
judgment on the quality of life we older Americans have passed
on to them. They are largely correct in their critique of the ways
we prowl the earth as hunters, our appetite for violence, our
cheap huckstering, our self-righteous foreign policies, our mil-
itarized universities, our racial arrogance, our hypocrisies about
sex and drugs, our concern with tranquillity shattered rather
than justice denied, and the insane distortions in our national
priorities. We are a generation of sleepwalkers and television-
viewers, and our kids have thrown cold water in our faces. I
bless them for shaking us awake to these realities.

But, right as their critique often is, their own prescriptions
are less than perfect. Most young people have copped out
themselves under cover of rhetoric (you can't change the system,
etc.), and some have taken the drug route to empty nirvana.
Many are so disenchanted they can't bear to read the newspapers. Despair is the ultimate cop out. A few have joined the
anti-democratic insurrectionaries, yielding themselves up to
mindless tactics of confrontationism. These youngsters may
help to bring on the rightist repression which is the greatest
danger facing America. We need to understand what is troubling
our young; we have no obligation to sign blank checks for
them or to rationalize their mistakes. They have no monopoly
on virtue, and social conscience is not correlated with age.
Some of the youngest, bravest, and most caring people I know
are in their fifties and sixties. The young sometimes have an
arrogance about them which is no lovelier than the arrogance
of the old. They do not know, as we know, of the immense
resiliency of America and its capacity to change when the
people truly will it.

And yet, I am fearful that—as America comes increasingly to
fear and hate the blacks and the poor who rattle our windows
and shatter our status quo—so may we also become a nation of
child-haters. Increasingly, as gorge rises, we are coming to scape-
goat the young (except the most housebroken), including our
own. No greater tragedy could befall us than to permit the
generational conflict to slide into mutual hostility and hatred.

So, as this book dealt frothily with ways to cope with young people, may I conclude with the most serious—and best—method of all: Work with them in building a just and decent society, a finer quality of life, and a gentle world. Let us together make our democratic system *produce!* Their hairdos and beards and flowers are mere symptoms; there are no ways to deal with symptoms except to go to the root causes—and these lie in the torments and agonies of our cities, our endless wars, our ravished environment, our racial shame, our disordered national purpose, our individual failings, our insensitivity. Against these obscenities we should be revolting with the kids. What they want most is to tame the savagery of man and make human the ways of the world. The Bible says: "Old men shall dream dreams —but our youth shall visions see." And thus it was millennia ago when God spoke of Abraham, the first Jew, the idol-smashing rebel: "I have loved him that he might command his children after him to keep the way of the Lord by doing justice and righteousness (Genesis 18:19)."